PORT

PORT

GEORGE ROBERTSON

FABER AND FABER
London & Boston

First published in 1978
by Faber and Faber Limited
3 Queen Square London WC1
Printed in Great Britain by
Latimer Trend & Company Ltd Plymouth
All rights reserved

British Library Cataloguing in Publication Data

Robertson, George
Port.—(Faber books on wine).
1. Port wine
I. Title
641.2'2   TP559.P58

ISBN 0-571-11023-1

Contents

This book is dedicated with deep affection to my wife, who has patiently shared her life with me and my other great love—port.

Preface

The production of port has been with us since the early eighteenth century. A quotation made by Richard Bentley at that time is worth recording: 'He is believed to have liked port, but to have said of claret, that it would be port if it could.' Need we say more? What finer appreciation of the qualities of port could we wish for?

No technical book has been written on port since Baron Forrester's thesis in the early nineteenth century. I feel that this is the moment to embark on one, a moment when mechanisation is pushing out all the older methods, many innovations have been implemented and stricter regulations enforced. I shall endeavour to blend the romantic background of the trade with a specific, factual, and educational story of port, coloured with a little history in order to understand it better.

I shall delve into this fascinating subject from its first inception until the present day, tracing each change and the reason for it as I go along. Most of my working life has been spent studying, tasting, blending and shipping port, and, not unnaturally, drinking it. It has always been, and is still, an integral part of my life.

As I sit writing this book, names of old wine trade friends, almost forgotten, flood in: the dozens who so readily passed on their vast knowledge of wines to me as the then younger member. The port trade has always been a close-knit community where competition spoils no friendships. We all have the same goal in view: the pleasure of producing port for all to enjoy. Thus we discuss its merits, glass in hand, sampling each drop, with what amounts almost to reverence, tasting, savouring and drinking the wine in order to increase our knowledge and train our palates.

How many pipes of port have trickled down our throats? I say trickled deliberately, as it is virtually impossible to gulp port. It is essentially a wine to be sipped and appreciated, and has mellowing properties. Even today, when conversation is fast becoming a lost art, port loosens the tongue and becomes in itself a conversation piece.

As a shipper, port is my life blood: I live it, with all its caprices, successes, failures, even tragedies. I breathe it and love it, and my aim is always to produce the quality to satisfy the consumer.

There are few terrains in the wine-growing world that are more mountainous, harder or tougher to cultivate than those of the Douro district. We say the Lord has given us the soil, the vine and the grape. Let us take advantage of them and produce high-quality port for all to enjoy. That is what this book is all about.

Acknowledgements

In preparing this book I have received a great deal of help from a number of friends and organisations connected with the port trade. I should particularly like to thank my colleague Robin Reid of Croft & Ca. Lda., in Portugal, for keeping me up to date with modern production and techniques; Julian Jeffs, Q.C., for his invaluable guidance and the editing of this book; Iain Macgregor for assiduously filling in the historical data; Engenheiro-Agrónomo Marques Gomes, Chief of the Technical Services in the Instituto do Vinho do Porto, and Alan Simpson, head of Research and Development, International Distillers and Vintners Ltd, for checking the manuscript dealing with diseases and viticulture; Cunnison Rankin and Stewart Reid of Rankin Brothers and Sons of London and Portugal, who ratified the chapter on cork; Engenheiro-Agrónomo Jose Barros of Pesinho, Douro, for the information on modern terracing and planting in the Douro region; The Port Wine Trade Association for the vintage port dates; The Instituto do Vinho do Porto for all their help over shipments and maps; Frederico Van Zeller of Quinta Noval-Vinhos (S.A.R.L.), for the information on his unique pre-*phylloxera* vines; and all my old Portuguese and British colleagues and friends, past and present, who taught me my viticulture, lodge work, cooperage, office work, analysis, tasting and blending. Although my old notebook is, in some cases, out of date, the basis of all my knowledge stems from this old relic dated 1935–7.

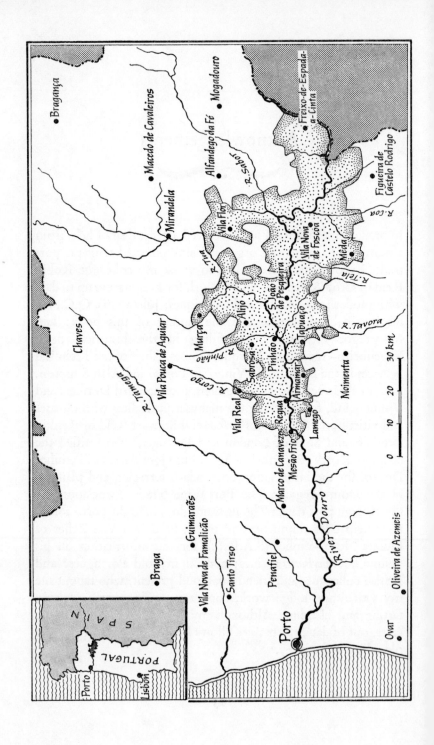

An Introduction to Port

What is port?

Port is a fortified wine grown in the wild and mountainous country of the Upper Douro in the north of Portugal in an officially demarcated area of approximately one thousand square miles, or 242,712 hectares. This area stretches from a point some sixty miles due east of Oporto at the mouth of the River Douro and follows the confluence of this river up to the Spanish frontier.

It is a wine, red or white, which has had its fermentation arrested at the time of the vintage with Portuguese brandy, or grape alcohol, which is produced from distilled Portuguese wines, usually from the south of the country where wine production is high. The arresting of the fermentation at the time of the vintage produces a medium-sweet wine in which some of the natural sugar content of the grape has been retained and the final sweetness is entirely controlled by the timing of the addition of this brandy (*aguardente*) at 77 per cent alcohol by volume in strength.

Before 1904 there was no legal definition of the name port in Great Britain. At the end of 1905 the British Foreign Office was approached by the port wine trade to rectify this, and the definition was finally agreed upon in the Anglo-Portuguese Commercial Treaty Acts of 1914 and 1916. The law states in Article 6 of the Treaty Act of 1914: 'His Britannic Majesty's Government engage to recommend to Parliament to prohibit the importation of any wine or other liquor to which the description "Port" or "Madeira" is applied other than the produce of Portugal and of the island of Madeira respectively.' The Act of 1916 states that port must be accompanied by a Certificate of Origin. In the United States of America the name was not protected until 1968 when the word 'Porto' was officially established and recognised as the fortified wine grown in the demarcated region of the upper Douro in the north of Portugal, and only that wine can bear the description of Porto.

The port trade has always been rather proud of the fact that its demarcated region in the upper Douro was officially established in 1756, one hundred years before the French controlled their wine-growing areas. In fact, the port-growing area was the first controlled one to be established anywhere.

The historical background

The story of Portugal has been chronicled by so many qualified (and unqualified!) historians, that we must try to confine our enthusiasm to those events which had at least some bearing on the wines from the north. If we often digress, our excuse will be that in any specialised treatment of history, there are vacuums which have to be filled.

The vine, according to most authorities, was first grown in Asia; but its introduction to Europe was not slow to follow. When it first reached Portugal will never precisely be known, but the first important date in the history of Portuguese viticulture is 1095. Two years previously, King Alfonso VI of Castile and Leon had arranged a marriage between his illegitimate daughter, Teresa, to Count Henry of Burgundy, who, perhaps for his tolerance of bastardy, was granted an earldom and extensive estates in Portugal. More important to that country's later prosperity, he brought with him many vines from his native country and planted them on his newly acquired lands in Leobriga—later to be named Guimaraens. The grapes were probably those which today bear the famous name of Pinot Noir, which the local peasants, with surprisingly diluted chauvinism, immediately restyled *Tinta da França*, or *Tinta Francisca* or *Francesa* ('French red') and the wines they made from them were far richer than the thin Galician wines they were currently producing.

Count Henry's county originally extended along the Atlantic Coast from the Minho to the Douro, the *'terra portugalensis'*, but Henry's far-sighted intervention in the Civil War, which broke out in the reign of Alfonso VI's successor and Henry's sister-in-law, Urraca, paid off handsomely. He, and later, his widow, Teresa, began extending their territory northwards into Galicia with the object of obtaining its independence. This policy was continued by their son, Alfonso, who progressively ennobled himself from Count to Duke, from Duke to Prince and finally to King, thus becoming the real founder of the Kingdom of Portugal. His nominal suzerain, Alfonso VII of Castile and Leon, reasonably taking exception to his cousin's self-aggrandisement, declared war on him in 1130 and seven years later forced him to make peace.

For the next six years the lesson seems to have had little effect on Alfonso of Portugal, who continued to maintain his independence and his Royal title. He stopped attending his suzerain's great councils and refused to join Alfonso of Castile in his campaigns against the Moors. In the end Alfonso VII of Castile, by the terms of the Treaty of Zamora, acknowledged his cousin's Royal status, a concession not confirmed by the Pope, who continued to address Alfonso I as Duke of Portugal, much to that social alpinist's disgust.

During the next century, King Alfonso I and his successors went on to enlarge their territories, capturing the Moorish strongholds of Lisbon and Cintra and later conquering the Algarve with the occasional, somewhat lethargic, help of German, Flemish and English Crusaders en route to the Holy Land and, eventually, the more sustained assistance of the Templars and the Knights Hospitallers of Santiago. The final conquest of the Algarve was accomplished by King Alfonso III in 1249. Throughout this time wine growing was steadily increasing and, following the surrender of the Moors, a trading treaty was established with England.

Alfonso III was an astute and liberal monarch, who did much

to increase his country's prosperity and to encourage industry, commerce and agriculture, particularly viticulture, within his realm. He was the first ruler to summon a parliament in Portugal, including representatives of the people, and to transfer his capital from Coimbra to Lisbon. Unfortunately, however, he extended his liberalism to his domestic life and in 1253, for obvious political advantages, married Beatrice of Castile. This would have been an astute move indeed, had not his first wife, Matilda of Boulogne, been very much alive! His bigamy resulted in his excommunication and a papal interdict, finally forcing him to abdicate in favour of his brother, Dom Denis.

King Denis continued his predecessor's encouragement of agriculture, turning vast areas of wasteland into fertile country and organising the first planting of vines in the Douro district. His cultivation was matched by his culture and, among his many intellectual enterprises, he established first in Lisbon, and later Coimbra, Portugal's first university, which is to this day the foremost academy of learning in the country.

His wife, Queen Isabel, was greatly loved for her care of the poor, but the enormous cost of her charity greatly worried the King. One day, the legend says she was distributing loaves to beggars when her husband unexpectedly found her. She tried desperately to hide the loaves under her cloak, but the King angrily ordered her to show him what she was hiding. As she opened her cloak, a cascade of roses fell to the ground. The miracle has been commemorated in paintings and statues throughout Portugal and the Queen was later canonised. History does not record what the beggars thought of this inedible transformation nor the King's reaction. Perhaps he anticipated and paraphrased Marie Antoinette's famous but entirely mythical remark: 'If they can't eat bread, let them eat roses!'

From the death in 1325 of 'O Lavrador' ('the husbandman'), the nickname so appropriately bestowed on King Denis, I must discipline myself against the temptation to recount in too much detail the fascinating history of Portugal for the next 330 years.

The long chapter of civil wars and dynastic struggles against Castile, which so crippled Portugal, did nothing to help the industrial and agricultural progress which Denis and his predecessors had initiated and so sedulously pursued. Denis's son, Alfonso IV, who seemed to have had a predilection for the Spanish way of life, led a revolt against his father, which sadly embittered that enlightened monarch's remaining years. At least Alfonso will be remembered from the viewpoint of the 'English connection' for the treaty he concluded with Edward III in 1353. This allowed the Portuguese to fish cod off the English coast in return for regular cargoes of wine, mostly from the Minho district and shipped in small casks and skins by Portuguese fishermen from the port of Viana do Castelo. That port became the centre of the international wine trade in the north of the country and its shippers can probably claim the distinction of being the first to introduce Portuguese wines in any quantity to England.

Alfonso's son, Pedro I, an impartial tyrant, is largely remembered for his belated disclosure of his secret marriage to Ines de Castro, who had already been quietly murdered by his father's henchmen. His reaction to his father's summary disposal of an unwanted daughter-in-law was to have her body exhumed from her tomb and the corpse crowned beside him at his coronation. A skeleton at the feast indeed!

What so often handicaps an historian and confuses his readers is the eternal duplication of names. Pedro I of Portugal is sometimes mistaken for the ineffable Pedro I of Castile and a little later we find confusion worse confounded by three major arbiters of Portugal's destiny, John I of Portugal, John I of Castile and England's John of Gaunt.

However in 1567, Pedro I of Portugal was succeeded by Ferdinand I, and it was this monarch who really demolished Portugal's peaceful industrial progress and agricultural development over the four reigns. On the unlamented death of Pedro I of Castile and the accession to his throne of the illegitimate, highly popular Henry of Trastamara, Ferdinand of Portugal unwisely claimed the Castilian throne on the somewhat shaky grounds that his grandmother had been Beatrice of Castile, the bigamous wife of Alfonso III. His claim was pursued throughout the reign of Henry of Trastamara and renewed on the accession to the Castilian throne of John I, thus involving his country in a whole series of wars against Castile, in which Portugal was several times invaded and her fertile lands largely devastated.

Throughout this long struggle the 'English connection' remained unbroken. Edward the Black Prince, Prince and Viceroy of Aquitaine, with his headquarters in Bordeaux, had had the bad taste to support Pedro the Cruel of Castile against Henry of Trastamara and in this he was ably assisted by his brother, John of Gaunt, Duke of Lancaster, who can certainly have had little choice in the matter. He had, for better rather than worse, married Pedro the Cruel's daughter, Blanche, and was using that right to compete against Ferdinand of Portugal as a claimant to the Castilian throne. Despite that rivalry, however, he remained a loyal friend and ally of Portugal, and on two occasions English troops and ships were sent to the help of that small and ailing country. Ferdinand later repaid that kindness by making peace with Castile without bothering to inform his English ally.

On his death in 1383, Ferdinand was succeeded by his daughter Beatrice, who had been married to King John II of Castile a few months earlier, with the object of uniting the two countries; but the people of Portugal had had enough. Always nationalistic to the point of xenophobia, they turned to John, illegitimate son of Pedro I of Portugal, and proclaimed him King, sending Beatrice and her Spanish husband packing. John I immediately renewed the alliance with England and enlisted a company of English archers (unsurpassed at that time throughout Europe as a fighting arm), who played an invaluable part in the battle of Aljubarrota, where John defeated a powerful Castilian army and assured the continued independence of Portugal. On the 9th May 1386, John concluded the Treaty of Windsor with the ill-fated Richard II of England. It was a pact of 'perpetual friendship' and an agreement to assist each other in all emergencies, probably the most enduring international alliance of all times.

Soon afterwards John cemented the alliance by marrying Philippa, the daughter of John of Gaunt and Blanche of Castile, delighting the ambitious Duke of Lancaster by renouncing all his rights to the throne of Castile and promising absolutely to back his father-in-law in that same objective. With the cynical faithlessness of princes, John of Gaunt eventually came to terms with John of Castile; but even that failed to disturb the Anglo-Portuguese alliance, which remained intact and was ratified in 1403 by Gaunt's son, Henry IV of England.

Philippa must have inherited the passion and strength of her father, for the fruits of her marriage rapidly approached the dimensions of an orchard. It was, however, her fourth son who was to be the inspiration and designer of Portugal's rise to the status of a world power in the next 300 years of her history. It was this son, later to be known throughout the world as Henry the Navigator, who began and fostered Portugal's expansionist programme of exploration overseas, who was the founder of Portugal's vast empire and the unwitting progenitor of his country's lasting impoverishment.

I used to think when I was a callow schoolboy in the 1920s that the world had been created by God for the British and that God was a Scotsman, or, at worst, an Englishman. Heretical defaulters like the Americans worried me a little; but the rash of red spots, like a global epidemic of measles, decorating my school atlas, would always set my chauvinistic mind at rest. It was therefore with a sense of outraged patriotism that I later discovered the extent of Portugal's empire in the fifteenth and sixteenth centuries and realised that the Portuguese explorers and empire-builders made our Hawkins, Drake and Raleigh look like weekend yachtsmen by comparison.

Cão, Covilhã, Diaz, Vasco da Gama, Fernandes, Barcellos, Cabot, the brothers Corte Real, Fernando Magalhães (better known as Magellan) and Cabral explored nearly all the oceans of the world. Among their many discoveries, conquests and explorations were Senegal, Cape Verde Islands, Sierra Leone,

Guinea, the Cape of Good Hope, Abyssinia, Calcutta, Madras, Goa, Ceylon, Malacca, the Spice Islands, Formosa, the Azores, Greenland and Labrador. In 1515 Portugal sent its first official mission to China and was allowed to settle a colony in Macao. Even Tibet was penetrated and the Nile explored. Small wonder that Camões declared: 'Had the world stretched farther, they would have gone there, too.' The greatest conquest of all, however, was Brazil, discovered in 1500 by Pedro Alvarez Cabral, a prize which was to play a major part in Portugal's political and economic future.

Self-styled 'intellectual liberals' (who are rarely either) always contend that 'empire' was synonymous with 'exploitation', a symbol of greed and ill-gotten pickings for the mother country. In the case of Portugal (and for that matter Rome, Spain and, eventually, Britain) imperial expansion was to lead to economic disaster. Instead of expanding their overseas trade, Portuguese magnates were busy importing the glamorous, unimagined produce of their New World. Thousands of Portuguese able-bodied men left home to join the expeditions overseas, leaving starving wives, children and old men to do what they could with the deserted factories and estates. The ever-increasing imports—mostly of luxury goods—resulted in an enormous national debt, while famine and plague decimated the remaining population. Portugal, despite or because of its empire, was practically bankrupt.

During this time various Portuguese monarchs continued to pursue their suicidal expansionist campaigns, and the final disaster came with the death and calamitous defeat of King Sebastian by the Moors at Alcazar-Quivir. He died without issue and no less than six claimants tried to seize the throne. The most important of these were Philip II of Spain, the grandson through his mother of Manuel I of Portugal and the Duchess of Bragança; but it was Antonio, a grandson, this time through his father, of Dom Manuel, whom the people of Portugal chose. Philip II immediately invaded Portugal and his army under the Duke of Alba soundly defeated Antonio at the Battle of Alcantara in 1580, virtually taking over the country and inaugurating what later became known as 'The Captivity'. Despite Philip's promise to guarantee Portugal's economy, the country was ruled for the next sixty years as a Spanish colony from Madrid. Enormous taxes were wrung from the long-suffering Portuguese and the revenues seized for the Spanish treasury.

During all this time, however, agriculture was miraculously sustained at the expense of industry. The vines in the Minho Province continued to flourish and, until the death of Sebastian, trade between England and Portugal was maintained and even increased, so much so that in 1578 an English consul was appointed in Viana do Castelo to protect English interests. It was perhaps unfortunate that this appointment coincided with the Battle of Alcazar-Quivir and the beginning three years later of 'The Captivity'; but despite Spain's hostility to England, culminating in 1588 in the destruction of the Armada, British factors came to settle in Viana and Monção, the wine-growing centre, and gradually spread their activities south-east to the Douro district.

Here it was soon discovered that, due to the superior quality of the soil, the wines it produced were 'bigger' and hardier (though less palatable) than any in the Minho Province. Rough, tough and durable, however, they could travel and that was good enough for the factors. Acres of wheat were forthwith turned over to vines and most of the wines were exported to England. The English meanwhile had considerably increased their fishing fleet and had perfected a new art in the curing of fish, which was greatly superior to the Portuguese methods. Now the Portuguese became the buyers of codfish from England and the growing English demand for wine promoted a two-way trade, greatly boosting shipments of Portuguese wines to our country.

During the sixty years of 'The Captivity' little is recorded of the activities of the English and Scottish merchant vintners in Portugal. This is not surprising, as one of Philip's first acts was to restrict their privileges. It is, however, known that during this time many of the fertile Minho lands were laid waste, forcing most of the British merchants to move to Oporto, which had apparently escaped the havoc of war.

England was in a difficult position. Deeply sympathetic to Portugal's plight as they were, it was impossible for the English ministers to consider her anything but a province of Spain and a tool for Philip II's aggression. When the Armada was finally launched from Lisbon, Portuguese ports were suspect and Elizabeth I had little alternative but to use the English Navy to cut the Portuguese trade routes. The English and Scottish factors (following James I's accession to the United Kingdom's throne in 1603, we can now call them 'British') must have suffered very hard times until the end of 'The Captivity' in 1640 and little is known of their activities or survival techniques during this period. It is probable that they spent some of their time surveying the Douro valley and assessing the quality and potentialities of its wines in preparation for an uncertain future.

The unrest among the Portuguese aristocracy finally came to a head when they refused an order from Olivares to help him quell a revolution in Catalonia. By December 1640 they were in open revolt against the Spanish hegemony, and soon proclaimed their leader, the Duke of Bragança, King as John IV. Encouraged by France and Cardinal Richelieu's tortuous anti-Spanish policies, King John set out to restore Portugal's fortunes and make peace with the other great powers. He did not have it all his own way. Two pro-Spanish plots to assassinate him failed and a further Spanish invasion was decisively defeated by Matheus de Albuquerque at Montijo in 1644. For twelve years his ailing son and successor, Alfonso VI, continued to resist successive Spanish attempts to regain the country and it was not until 1668 that, by the Treaty of Lisbon, Spain finally recognised Portugal's independence.

Throughout 'The Captivity' the British and Dutch had begun to challenge Portugal's sea-power, taking advantage of her enforced union with Spain to invade her colonies. The English attacked Pernambuco and the Azores, devastating both, and then started to dispute the Portuguese monopolies in India; the Dutch drove the Portuguese from Malacca and captured many of Portugal's possessions in India and Ceylon. Formosa and, with it, much of Portugal's trade with China, was also lost. In

1654, therefore, John IV, to protect his rapidly vanishing Empire, concluded new treaties and trade agreements with Cromwell, which were ratified after the Stuart restoration by Alfonso signing a treaty with Charles II, following the latter's marriage to Alfonso's sister, Catherine of Bragança. Catherine's dowry included the cession to Charles of Tangier, the port of Galle in Ceylon, and Bombay; doubtless some compensation to Charles for his temporary post-marital separation from his many mistresses.

These treaties also granted the British merchants in Portugal special privileges, which so favoured them that they were soon more powerful and prosperous than the Portuguese traders themselves. According to John Croft, in his *Treatise on the Wines of Portugal*, published in 1788, the privileges enabled the British merchants to form their first 'Factory' or association of British traders in Oporto and, although they still dealt mainly in cotton, wheat and salted fish, a profitable wine business was still being run from Viana.

Most Portuguese monarchs seem to have been curiously misguided in their choice of brides, and Alfonso VI was no exception. After an unfortunate matrimonial venture he was deposed and imprisoned until his death in 1683. The Regent, his brother, succeeded him as Pedro II and it was during his reign that relations with Britain drew even closer.

Between 1678 and 1685 Britain had placed an embargo on trade with its principal rival and enemy, France. In the former year, only about 120 tuns* of Portuguese wine were imported into London, but this figure quickly rose to 6,880 tuns average shipment during the period of the embargo. It is doubtful, however, where all this wine came from: the figures are notoriously unreliable, and a good deal of it may have been French wine masquerading as Portuguese, exported from Bordeaux via Oporto. And with the end of the embargo in 1685 the pre-eminence of French wine was immediately restored, while that of the Portuguese collapsed at once. War broke out with France again, however, in 1689 and again there was an

* A tun was equal to two pipes: i.e. 230 gallons

embargo against French wine. The real trade in Portuguese wine dates from this time, and the figures are much more reliable, as those of imports into London correspond reasonably closely with those of exports from Portugal. The average import into London between 1690 and 1696 was 5,440 tuns while the exports from Oporto during the same period amounted to 4,660 tuns. The import figures may include some French wines wrongly described, but some of the difference would be accounted for by genuine Portuguese wines exported from other ports. London at this time was handling 88 per cent of the trade in Portuguese wines, despite the fact that lower rates of duty were payable at other ports. For this reason the proportion of the trade handled by London gradually declined thereafter. There can be no doubt that the bulk of Portuguese wine sold at this time was genuine. In 1697, French wines were allowed in again, but the duty on them had been raised drastically to £53 1s 0d a tun, while Portuguese wines paid only £22 12s 0d.* For this reason the trade in French wines remained minimal while that in Portuguese wines went from strength to strength, encouraged by the long-term security provided by the Methuen Treaty. The duties were varied from time to time in the course of the century, but the preferential duty in favour of Portugal was retained until 1786. Although Spanish wines paid little more duty than did Portuguese, repeated wars between Spain and England, together with grossly bad organisation of the wine trade in the most directly competitive Spanish area of Jerez, prevented the Spaniards from taking advantage of it†. Nor was Spain in a position to provide high-quality red wines, which were most in demand.

In May 1703 a further Anglo-Portuguese treaty was signed by Sir Paul Methuen, allowing England to invade Spain through Portugal during the War of the Spanish Succession. That treaty must not be confused with the famous Methuen Treaty of December 1703, signed by the British Envoy, John Methuen, Sir

* For these figures, and much other valuable information in this chapter, we are indebted to H. E. S. Fisher's valuable *The Portugal Trade* (Methuen, 1971)

† For further details, see *Sherry* by Julian Jeffs, published in this Series

Paul's father, which granted preferential treatment to Portuguese wine exports to Britain and reciprocal preference for British textiles into Portugal. This highly significant trade treaty marked from the British point of view a turning point in the Portuguese wine industry.

Despite controversy over the real benefits to both countries of the Methuen Treaty, the date of its signing will always be regarded as a red-letter day by all lovers of wine. Portugal had for the previous six years been enjoying in Britain a far more favourable rate of duty for her wines than any other country. There was, therefore, nothing particularly new about the treaty's provision that Portuguese wines should pay one-third less duty than French wines. Nor did the preferential provision covering the import of English woollens into Portugal do much good for the Portuguese textile industry, which was almost bankrupted by the unwelcome competition. What it did do for the Oporto shippers and growers was to give them a secure and valuable market in Britain and the hope of a bright enough future for them to pursue the years of expensive research and experimentation which were to climax in the superb fortified wines we know today.

For the Portuguese, the treaty seemed to free them from Franco-Spanish domination, giving them that sense of security they badly needed. They overlooked the fact that it virtually made Portugal a satellite of Britain and, in fact, lost for their country a considerable amount of trade in goods other than wine. The treaty had also given Britain valuable trading rights with Brazil. That country had always before shipped its produce to Portugal for re-export to Britain, and those re-export profits were now lost to Portugal. Brazil had at last grown up and left its mother for good.

It was about this time that the Douro growers decided to experiment with the fortification of their coarse and somewhat unappetising *consumo* wines. In 1678 two young English gentlemen were sent to Portugal to learn the wine trade and find wines suitable for the British markets. While calling at a monastery in Lamego, near the River Douro, they were royally entertained by the abbot, who served them a wine entirely new to them called Pinhão. They found it slightly sweet, very smooth and surprisingly palatable. After persuading them to buy a substantial quantity, the abbot confided to them that he had added several litres of local brandy to the cask during fermentation, thus conserving the natural sugar of the grape. He had in fact taken the basic idea of fortification from Spain; but his guests were decidedly intrigued. They added still more brandy to their purchase, not to improve it (which it certainly did not) but to help preserve it on its long voyage to England. They not only succeeded in that intention, but virtually laid the foundation-stone of what we now call port.

The abbot, however, must have been ahead of his time. More usually then (and for a long time after) brandy was added to the wine *after* fermentation was complete. Only later did the wine-makers of Oporto learn to use brandy to arrest fermentation and thus produce a medium-sweet fortified wine. It was probably soon after this time, in about 1730, that fortification came into general use, producing the kind of wines that we know today. In the early years of the century, the wine exported had been only about a year old, but the fortified wines needed longer to mature and the age at export was soon doubled or trebled. This in turn led to the need for far more working capital, and favoured the British merchants, so that the trade became vested almost entirely in their hands.

From 1703 onwards the Upper Douro wine industry developed rapidly, taking advantage of the bonanza the Methuen Treaty had inspired. Countless acres of grain were converted into vineyards, to the great advantage of the merchants and the semi-starvation of the peasants, whose staple diet had to be sacrificed for the benefit of the export trade. Portugal became more and more an agricultural nation and less a producer of raw materials, and its birth as an industrial country was deferred for well over a century, when the Methuen Treaty was finally revoked by mutual agreement in 1842.

The effect of the treaty on the import of French wines to England can well be imagined. On the accession of William and Mary and the succeeding policy of total war on France, the French wine industry was close to ruin. According to Mr Warner Allen, the extra £8 a tun clapped on French wine was disastrous. In 1672 the French exported to Britain 22,000 tuns of wine; by 1697 their total shipments amounted to '2 tuns, 2 hogsheads and 18 gallons'.

There appeared at this time an often-quoted advertisement in London's *Daily Courant* of January 1712:

'The first loss is the best, specially in the Wine Trade, and upon that consideration Mr John Crooke will now sell his French Claret at 4s 0d a gallon, to make an end of a troublesome and losing trade. Dated the 7th of January from his vault in Broad Street. . . .'

Selling his 'Claret' at eightpence a bottle makes one wonder whether Mr Crooke was a dedicated patriot, an idiot, or merely living up to his name.

In the same publication was a superb announcement which today would have been grist to Mr Cyril Fletcher's mill:

'. . . advertiser making advantageous purchase offers for sale on very low terms about six dozen of prime Port Wine, late the property of a gentleman of forty years of age, full in body and with a very high bouquet.'

Obesity *and* halitosis, poor fellow? Or, as Mr Warner Allen suggests, if 'the forty years of age' applied to the wine and not the gentleman, only the shift of a comma would oblige us to antedate by many years our hypothetical date for the birth of vintage port.

Warner Allen in his fascinating book, *A History Of Wine*, also reminds us of Swift's patriotic appeal to the British people:

Be sometimes to your Country true,
Have once the public good in view:
Bravely despise Champagne at Court
And choose to dine at home with Port.

Swift's lamentable doggerel can be forgiven more easily than his duplicity, for in the same year he is writing to Stella confessing the limitations of his palate: 'I love White Portuguese Wine better than Claret, Champagne or Burgundy; I have a sad, vulgar appetite.' But Swift's tacit admission of the inferiority of Portuguese wines to French was a commonly held opinion. It was easier to import Portuguese wines to Britain than to sell them. Despite the scarcity of French wines, English gentlemen of taste and fashion would sacrifice patriotism for *gourmandise* whenever they could find a claret, and, as we shall see, it was not very long before the Oporto shippers began to feel the pinch. It is, therefore, high time we returned to Portugal.

Pedro II was succeeded in 1706 by John V, whose reign was chiefly renowned for its profligacy. Gold and precious stones flooded into Portugal from Brazil and were squandered in wasteful extravagance by the rich and the noble, who tried to outdo even Louis XIV in their manic demand for bigger and more luxurious palaces and mansions. Meanwhile, the poor grew poorer, and thousands emigrated to find their mythical Eldorados overseas. The effect on Portuguese agriculture was catastrophic and the accession of Joseph I in 1750 only brought worse calamities. Five years after his accession, two-thirds of the city of Lisbon was reduced to rubble by a disastrous earthquake.

The only compensation for a national disaster is that it often reveals the right man in the right place to salvage the country's fortunes. Sebastian Carvalho e Melo, Marquess of Pombal, was such a man. The calm and immaculate efficiency with which he handled the crisis following the earthquake earned him the unlimited power of a dictator. King Joseph made him his chief minister and one of his first acts was to found a board of trade, which, under his autocratic direction, virtually took over control of the Douro wine trade.

The establishment of a steady trade led, of course, to the foundation of many more merchant houses. Some, however, predate the boom. C. N. Kopke & Co Ltd claims to be the oldest, with a foundation date of 1638; founded by a German, and once English owned, it is now Portuguese. Warre & Co claims to have been founded in 1670, and Croft & Co is almost as ancient, dating from 1678: the publication of this book coincides with its tercentenary. Other firms soon followed:

Quarles Harris, 1680; Taylor, Fladgate Yeatman, 1692; Morgan Bros, 1715; Offley Forrester, 1729; Butler & Nephew, 1730; Hunt Roope, 1735; Sandeman, 1790; Graham, 1814; Cockburn, 1815; Feuerheerd, 1815; Guimaraens, 1822; Silva & Cosens, 1862; Delaforce, 1868; and so on. But such a list must be looked at with caution: in the early days, many of the firms dealt in wine only as a sideline, if at all. And some of their histories are largely based on secondary sources which we have found very unreliable. To prepare a history of port in terms of the individual Houses would be a daunting task—if, indeed, possible—as many essential documents have long since been destroyed.

In 1727 British wine shippers in Oporto had formed an Association to regulate and improve their trade by the simple method of forcing down the prices paid to the wine farmers. This, of course, only served to create further poverty for the peasants and did little or nothing to improve the factors' overseas trade. The power of the Association, however, was immense, and, until the intervention of Pombal, practically unrestricted.

In 1755 an enterprising Spaniard by the name of Pancorbo founded what was called in English the 'Oporto Wine Company'. The combined opposition of the British Association of traders at once assured the failure of Pancorbo's initiative. A year later Pombal decided that enough was enough. His reaction was to limit through the board of trade the privileges enjoyed by the British merchants since the treaties of 1654 and 1661. The following year he re-established the Oporto Wine Company to handle exclusively the wines of the Upper Douro. By this act he could control the port trade and restrict the area of wine production. His laudable intention was to override the conservative methods of the British factors by improving and controlling the quality of the wine, with a view to resuscitating the dying export trade.

The British factors in Oporto had no one but themselves to blame. For years they had waged a running battle with the growers, dictating to the latter how the wines should be made.

The growers had already discovered the secret of adding brandy to the wine during fermentation to check the latter's growth; but unfortunately the very 'green' wines they were using, and the inferior quality of the brandy, made the resulting blend highly unpleasant. For economy reasons they were merely adding ten to fifteen litres of brandy per pipe, which arrested fermentation only temporarily and on re-fermentation made the wines almost undrinkable.

The British factors were furious. Sharing the blindness of the wine merchants in Britain, they had yet to visualise the final destiny of the Douro wines and their eventual transformation from inferior table wines to delicious dessert wines. In 1754 the factors wrote to their agents in the Upper Douro:

'The grower at the time of the Vintage, is in the habit of checking the fermentation of the wines *too soon* [my italics], by putting brandy into them while still fermenting; a practice which must be considered DIABOLICAL, for after this the wines will not remain quiet, but are continually tending to ferment and to become ropy and acid.'

The agents replied that it was 'proper to dash the wine with brandy in the fermentation to give it strength; with elderberries or the rind of ripe grape to give it colour. . . .' They went on to admit that the 'prescription' increased the cost of the wine and that British wine merchants were still complaining of 'a lack of colour, strength and maturity in the article supplied'. The dissatisfaction of their British customers spurred the growers to propagate even more fantastic recipes, until the wine became 'a mere confusion of mixtures'. It will surprise no one that by the use of such methods, the situation of the Douro wine industry soon became desperate. The wines were atrocious and most British wine-lovers refused to drink them. Even the callow palates of the boys at Eton were outraged and they soon coined a name for the concoction, 'black-strap', which derisive label was in common use for some years.

The re-establishment of the Oporto Wine Company by Pombal was a much needed 'stitch in time'. His decrees, though unpopular with the British Association, factors and growers alike, were eminently desirable. Not only did he restrict the wine-growing areas and ban the use of elderberries, but he forbade the use of manure in the cultivation of the vines, measures which, while reducing the quantity, greatly improved the quality of the wines produced. Finally, he gave the Oporto Wine Company the exclusive right to distil grape brandy to add to the wines, and the brandy it made was far superior to the fiery spirit the growers had been using before.

Had Pombal's genius been given a free rein for a few more years, the discovery of port as the perfect dessert wine might not have been so long postponed. The Portuguese, however, are nothing if not individualists and any kind of arbitrarily imposed reform was anathema to them. The Marquess was no believer in hidebound democracy and his ideas, though mostly admirable, were inevitably rejected by the people. Anti-reform riots, almost certainly encouraged by the merchants, broke out in Oporto in 1757. These Pombal savagely repressed, only enlarging the formidable list of his enemies. His dictatorship might well have come to an earlier end, had not a new war with Spain begun in 1762, when Portugal refused to accede to Spanish demands to close her ports against Britain.

A large Spanish army invaded the country, scoring initial successes at Bragança and Almeida. Lisbon itself was in imminent danger of capture when the Spaniards were stopped and forced to retreat by a combined force of British and Portuguese. A peace between Spain and Britain in 1763 ensured the withdrawal of all Spanish forces from Portugal.

The war probably saved Pombal. People's minds were otherwise engaged and a man of the Marquess's calibre was still needed to rebuild the Portuguese postwar economy and credit. This remarkable man continued to manage his country's affairs for another fourteen years, and it was not until King Joseph's death in 1777 and his daughter Maria's accession that Pombal fell from power. Joseph had always refused to listen to his detractors, who soon turned to his impressionable, unbalanced daughter for sympathy. The poison worked. Maria's first act was to pardon and free many of Pombal's political prisoners, who in their turn persuaded the Queen that he had consistently abused his powers. In the same year she dismissed him and confiscated all his powers and privileges. At eighty-three he was too old and disillusioned to fight both his enemies and an inexperienced, prejudiced Queen. He was subjected to three months' interrogation, found guilty and banished by the Queen from Lisbon, retiring, a broken man to Pombal, where he died five years later. Whatever history's verdict, there is no doubt that the Oporto wine trade will always owe a heavy, if unrecognised, debt to the Marquess of Pombal.

The relaxation of the wine laws following Pombal's disgrace merely meant an increase in the quantity of wine made and shipped and an inevitable drop in quality; but the Oporto Wine Company at least remained. Although it failed in its attempt to gain a total monopoly of the trade, it was responsible for many improvements and innovations, not the least of which was to make the dangerous reaches of the River Douro navigable. The project took twelve years to complete and in the end even the treacherous rapids of the Cachão Valeira, where many cargoes had been lost, had been secured for shipping.

Far and away the most important innovation was the gradual modifications in the shape of the wine bottle. Originally squat and bulbous, it was impossible to lay it on its side for binning. The cork, never being in contact with the wine, would dry and shrink, forming an air bubble in the bottle neck, which provided a comfortable sanctuary for hostile micro-organisms. No wonder the English consumers found that the wines were either oxidised or tasted like vinegar.

It was not until 1758 that the body of the bottle was contracted; but, as the neck was made even longer, the bottle still proved impossible to bin. Finally in 1775 an elongated bottle was evolved. It had a longer, thinner body and shorter neck, which made binning a practical proposition and enabled the wine to stay in contact with the cork. This, wrote André Simon in his *Bottle-screw Days*, resulted in the final development in about 1784 of the bottle which has been the standard port bottle ever since. Warner Allen, however, made the point in his book

Sherry and Port, that it was the year 1775 which saw the production of 'the first wine which could worthily claim the title Vintage Port'.

From this time until the outbreak of the French Revolution the port trade's fortunes improved immeasurably. By 1792 shipments to Britain had reached a record total of 50,000 pipes; but six years before that the factors' euphoria was enough to justify laying the foundation-stone in Oporto of the famous Factory House. There is nothing in Portugal to match this magnificent granite mansion, originally built as a centre for the British traders and factors dealing in every kind of commodity, but later taken over entirely by the port wine shippers, who still run it today. An exclusive British club? A conference centre? A chamber of commerce? Precisely! It was, and is, all of these things and none of them, an inexplicable paradox which can only be understood if you have the luck to be invited to luncheon there by one or other of the member firms. Its rightful name is 'The British Association'; its popular name now and for the past 177 years is the Factory House, and may it long remain so.

The French Revolution was at once a blessing and a curse for the Oporto wine trade. On the one hand, Britain was once again at war with France and French wine exports dropped to nothing. On the other hand, Portugal was in turmoil, the loyalties of her people evenly divided between the French revolutionaries and the British. Discontent was general and disciplinary measures hardly facilitated by the insanity, from 1792 until her death, of Queen Maria I. Her son and heir to the throne, Prince John, was made Regent, but he seems to have been a vacillating type, who lacked the personality or the strength of will to control his country's destiny. First Portugal allied herself with Spain against France and in 1793 sent an army to the Pyrénées. Later, Spain, anticipating by nearly a century and a half Mussolini's Italy as the jackal of Europe, made peace with France and war with Britain. In 1796 she was secretly negotiating with Napoleon Bonaparte the partition of Portugal.

When Napoleon offered Prince John a humiliating peace,

Portugal called for and received help from Britain in the form of troops and a subsidy. It was not enough. Spain launched a sudden invasion, forcing from Prince John territorial concessions and the payment of an indemnity to France under the terms of the Peace of Badajoz in 1801. For six years thereafter Portugal remained an uneasy neutral, awaiting the next inevitable onslaught. It came in 1807 when Napoleon concluded a treaty with Spain at Fontainebleau, partitioning Portugal, and sent an army under Marshal Junot to invade the virtually defenceless victim of Spanish treachery.

It should of course have been a walk-over; but the Emperor, like many other European tyrants before and since, had underestimated Britain and, in particular, one young and brilliant British commander by the name of Arthur Wellesley.

In no time at all Junot's triumphant army had overrun Portugal and captured Lisbon. The British government had, however, anticipated that initial success by persuading the Regent, Prince John, his mother and the Court to escape in plenty of time to Brazil. The decks were cleared, and in 1808 Sir Arthur Wellesley landed with a small army in Portugal. Thus began the Peninsular War and three years of peril for Portugal.

Almost immediately Wellesley (later of course to be Duke of Wellington) defeated Junot brilliantly at Vimieiro. The French marshal hardly knew what had hit him, and his humiliation and that of French arms in general was scarcely mollified by the condescending courtesy with which, under the Convention of Cintra, he and his troops were permitted to return unmolested and with the honours of war to France.

Junot in disgrace was replaced by the very able Marshal Soult, rated second only to the Emperor in generalship. In March 1809 he re-invaded Portugal and, among other successes, captured Oporto. Wellesley was ordered to return and, landing this time at Lisbon, advanced by forced marches to the Douro. Assisted by the Portuguese resistance movement in Oporto, he arrived at Vila Nova de Gaia, just opposite the city on the south side of the River Douro, taking Soult completely by surprise. The French were routed and Oporto recaptured. Retreating in disorder to Spain and pursued all the way by Wellington, they finally regrouped to meet the British and were soundly defeated at Talavera.

Napoleon, still unable to believe in Wellington's superior military genius, and convinced only that the British general had had more than his fair share of luck, sent yet another of his marshals to invade Portugal in 1810. Wellington was back in England and Marshal Masséna was certain this time that he had nothing to worry about. He was wrong. Britain had more than one brilliant commander.

In Wellington's absence, General Lord Beresford had been training and arming a very capable Portuguese army. Under Beresford's inspiring leadership the Portuguese met and contained with notable valour Masséna's sustained attacks, giving Wellington the much-needed time to return and defeat the French at Bussaco. Masséna, however, was quickly reinforced and in still superior strength remained a continuing danger. Wellington's choice of strategy was, as always, unexpected, unorthodox and, to the enemy at least, incomprehensible. He withdrew south towards Lisbon.

Masséna should have been aware of the adage: 'lead them on; wear them down and destroy them;' but his intelligence was incomplete. Unknown to the French, the British had secretly constructed a heavily fortified defensive line at Torres Vedras to protect Lisbon. Wellington retired fast, but in excellent order, to entrench his army behind this impregnable fortress. His strategy as always was immaculately successful. Masséna launched his troops again and again at the Torres Vedras lines, suffering appalling losses with each repulse. There was no disputing the gallantry of his infantry; but an army lives on its stomach and Wellington's scorched-earth policy in front of Torres Vedras meant that only an early penetration of the defences could save the French.

That was not to be. Masséna was beaten before he began. Hunger and disease inflicted even severer losses on his army, finally compelling him to evacuate all his positions and retire ignominiously to Spain. Economically exhausted and at a terrible cost to her people and environment, Portugal, the soul of courage, had again won her independence.

Civil war disrupted trade still further in 1827, and but for the arrival in 1831 of James Forrester, who knows what fate might not have befallen the port trade? Inseparable from the history of port is the name of this gentleman, who was born in 1809 in England and went out to Oporto to join his uncle in 1831 in the already established wine firm of Offley, Webber and Forrester. In 1836 he married Elisa Cramp, sister of another partner in the company, who bore him six children and died in 1847 at an early age.

James Forrester became something of a legend in Portugal, even in his lifetime. He was educated in the public-school tradition of England and was very gifted, being extremely artistic, sketching and painting exceptionally well, as well as delving into architecture and taking tremendous interest in the old Portuguese buildings. At the same time, he was an outstanding cartographer, in fact, it was scarcely possible to believe his superbly drawn maps were all hand-drawn, so professional were they, as well as his collection of portraits of outstanding personalities in and out of the port trade. Not only was he very scholarly, but also an elegant and charming man who added much to any social gathering. He entertained freely in his own home in Vila Nova de Gaia and never became involved in politics.

On his arrival in Oporto he immediately set out to learn the language. His fascination for his work as a producer and shipper of port led him to a detailed study of everything concerned with this subject. He drew an accurate geographic map of Oporto; hydraulic and topographical maps of the River Douro and especially good topographical ones of the wine area of the Alto Douro; a geographical map of the bed and margins of the same river, and soundings of the bed of the river from its mouth in Oporto to Barca d'Alva, the town on the Portuguese-Spanish border. He wrote endless theses on every aspect of port production and printed them. His essay on pests and diseases of the vine, brilliantly illustrated in colour, was adopted by the Royal Society in London. He did not limit himself to the vine but also wrote and illustrated a complete collection of all the cereals, vegetables and fruits of the Douro, not forgetting the all-important olive, and he invented an improved method of extracting olive oil. Finally he made a collection of earthenware figures representing regional costumes used at that period, which amounted to about four hundred, a different one from every possible village and district in Portugal.

This great man, loved by all, rich and poor, kings and noblemen, warring politicians, farmers and labourers alike, met an untimely end in the River Douro he loved so much. In May 1861, visiting his millionaire friend, Snr Silva Torres in his famous Quinta do Vezuvio, a river trip was organised. The river was in full spate after several days of heavy rain, and while manoeuvring the boat through the dangerous rapids of the Cachão da Valeira, the boat hit a rock which split open one of the seams and it sank. Unfortunately, the mast hit the Baron and though he endeavoured to swim ashore, he was unduly hampered by his leather money-belt laden with the wages for his farmers, and fatigued with his injury, he drowned. Some have suggested that he was drowned on purpose so that the gold could be stolen, but there is no reason to believe that this was so. The ladies in the boat were wearing crinolines, which was the dress of the day, and were kept afloat by their hoops acting as life-jackets.

With the death of Forrester, the port trade lost not only one of its greatest ambassadors but also one of the most knowledgeable men of that time. Luckily, he left behind him countless erudite writings and sketches which are invaluable to our trade, even to this day.

These were unsettled days in Portugal, when bandits attacked and set fire to the wine lodges in Gaia, causing the wine to flow down the streets into the River Douro like streams of blood. The Oporto Wine Company, once more unpopular, was deprived of all its rights and dissolved after operating off and on for seventy-eight years. A free-for-all followed and a period of free trade ensued, resulting in complete chaos and confusion. For four years this state of affairs continued, back once more to the adulteration of wine with the elderberry for colour and sugar for sweetness, making the wine unpalatable and causing bankruptcies among many producers and farmers.

Queen Maria II of Portugal reinstated the Oporto Wine Company once again in 1838, but with fewer rights. The government subsidised it in order that they might purchase the surplus wines made, which were then auctioned in Regua. Although this Company, attempting to monopolise the wine trade, served many useful purposes, including the control of the export of port to Great Britain and the elimination of various irregularities in the production of the wine, it became progressively more unpopular and was finally, once and for all, liquidated in 1858. Despite the misgivings of the shippers, during the ten years from 1850 to 1860, the trade continued to expand and prosper.

In 1868, tragedy struck; no more devastating happening has ever caused such a blow to the wine trade in the Douro. This single blow was the arrival of the *phylloxera* beetle. Originating in the United States of America, it invaded the vineyards and virtually destroyed them throughout the whole country. This malady will be dealt with in context in the chapter dealing with the vines later on. Suffice it to say here that a remedy was available: grafting the native vines on to American stocks, which were resistant to it. Eleven years later, the American vine stock was in general use, and five years after that, in 1884, came the turning point of the port trade.

In 1872 the Portuguese government, resenting the profits made by the British shippers and the privileges they still enjoyed, had attempted once more to form a monopoly. In their terms, one could alas see, politics were the driving force. Far from ensuring the wholesomeness and genuineness of port, the shippers realised the innuendoes in the draft could have indeed the opposite effect and cause defamation of port, with subsequent alienation of the consumer. Therefore, the British shippers, backed by the Douro farmers, objected in no mean terms, and throughout the wrangling, disruptions in the trade were once again considerable. The King of Portugal was asked to intervene, but unfortunately this had little effect.

Thus the shippers closed their lodges in Gaia, and close on their heels, the lightermen refused to handle, load or unload the wines, causing chaos due to the mounting stocks of port stacked on the riverside and in the lodges themselves. Lord Salisbury, the then British Foreign Minister, telegraphed the King and requested an intervention once more; at the same time a commission was set up in Oporto of shippers fighting for their cause. The military were called in on the Portuguese civil governor's behalf, and feelings ran so high that the Government petitioned His Majesty to adjourn Parliament in order to cool down the tension and stave off what was likely to have turned into a revolution. Fortunately, a face-saving operation finally put paid to the ill-fated Company on a legal point. It was officially declared null and void, since ninety days had passed without its ratification.

A cholera epidemic swept the country in 1899 and regulations brought in to check the plague hampered the port trade once more. A 'sanitary cordon' was established and no one knew how he would reach the Douro district for the vintage; but luckily the health checks and disinfection were so piecemeal, and the epidemic was anyhow dwindling, that by August no one took any further notice of these checks and the workers were able to continue with the vintage, passing freely from their houses to the vineyards.

The year 1907 saw the loss of the heretofore prosperous Russian market. The Russians bought large quantities of the most expensive white ports but their government, wishing to promote their own domestic wines, imposed the exorbitant duty of £60 per pipe on port with the inevitable result that all shipments to that country ceased.

One of the worst floods of the River Douro occurred in 1909, when the water rose to such a height that the bridge between Oporto and Gaia was impassable. The wine-lodges were inundated, untold damage to the structure of the lodges added to the crises, and even the railway could not function as parts of it were flooded. Many thousands of pounds' worth of damage was caused and an incalculable quantity of port was lost, as well as steamers, fishing boats and building materials, which littered the banks of the river.

When the lodges were just beginning to recover from this disaster, the world plunged into the 1914 war. This terrible conflict took place far from the port wine country, but there was an inevitable reduction of shipments of port, partly due to restrictions, and not a little to the greatly increased war-risk insurance on each shipment. At least one bright spot, however, marked this year: the Anglo-Portuguese Commercial Treaty was signed, establishing the legal definition of port. This was followed in 1916 by legislation stating that all port shipped or exported must be accompanied by a Certificate of Origin.

Despite the jubilations and celebrations at the ending of the First World War, the port trade was not happy, owing to the discontent of the lodgemen and coopers, who came out on strike in 1919 and severely reduced the profits of that year. But round the corner in the 1920s came the port boom. Never had the demand been higher; the annual world shipments rose to 95,000 pipes, and this despite the French, Russian and Norwegian markets remaining closed to port.

Unfortunately for port, the trends in British habits began to change in the late 1920s, when cocktail parties and sherry parties became the vogue and the draught began to be keenly felt among the port shippers. In fact, in the mid-twenties, port was considered more and more in the British market as a dessert wine with a resultant lower demand. However, it is interesting to note that in the mid-1930s 80 per cent of the 40,000 pipes shipped to Great Britain was drunk as 'port and lemon', which meant that the pub trade was still booming.

Fortunately, the French at this time had begun to drink port as an apéritif, and shipments to France increased by leaps and bounds. Nearly 9,000 pipes were shipped in 1936 alone, and the fashion there had come to stay; by 1963 France had ousted Great Britain as the leading port importer, and she still maintains that position today, shipping one-third of the total production.

Control of port and protection for the shippers was a growing necessity, and thus in 1933 the Portuguese government established three main bodies to supervise and control the trade. These were the Instituto do Vinho do Porto, the Casa do Douro and the Gremio dos Exportadores do Vinho do Porto. These establishments will be dealt with in more detail later in the chapter.

During the 1930s there was a very real threat to the continued existence of vintage ports, and one that was happily averted. The world slump had drastically reduced the demand so that very little of the great 1931 vintage was shipped at all. The duty was high, and the Port Wine Trade Association approached the Board of Customs and Excise and obtained the concession that port could be bottled in bond. They achieved this just in time for the great 1935 vintage. One result was that port was bottled more often by the shippers and less often by the merchants.

The 1939–45 war virtually brought the port trade to a standstill as shipments were on strict quota, it being a luxury commodity. The chain reaction of this scarcity was felt by the trade for some time after the war, as a whole generation of young had grown up with virtually no knowledge of this product, having neither seen nor tasted it. Unfortunately, too, there were too many ridiculous stories of the 'old Colonel' and gout attached to this wine which naturally gave them the wrong impression, though the medical profession had already learnt that port is not the cause of gout. Hence the sad fall in demand; but thankfully today, with a certain amount of 'education', the taste is returning, and who knows, maybe soon the British will again achieve their original position as the great port drinkers of the world!

From 1950 to the present day, gradual changes have come over the port trade. A slow but steady mechanisation programme and modern marketing techniques and the export of brands in bottle from Portugal all add up to progress. This short chapter on the history of port will give the reader an idea of the ups and downs of the trade over a period of relatively few years, and it shows that very little will deter the producer from searching and, indeed, fighting for the final product, whatever natural or man-made hazards may arise. Modern ways of life bring more and more people of different nations to Portugal to see how port is made, and taste this superb wine of the Douro. This in itself will surely promote an ever increasing demand for it.

Of the more recent political turmoils we shall say nothing, for stability has not yet returned and it will be some years before they can be judged objectively, either in the context of Portuguese history or in that of the port trade.

Government departments and local associations

The Portuguese government has devoted a great deal of attention to the authenticity and quality of port, and in June 1933 established a complete and efficient system of control from the vine to the glass. The system comprises three bodies controlling the port wine trade, as a whole, in Portugal—the Instituto do Vinho do Porto (the Port Wine Institute), the Casa do Douro (the Farmers' and Wine Growers' Association) and the Gremio dos Exportadores do Vinho do Porto (the Port Wine Shippers' Association).

The Instituto do Vinho do Porto is the official government body which controls the other two, the Casa do Douro and the Gremio. This organisation examines, directs and controls the production and trading of port. It employs inspectors to control the entry, exit and storing of port in the entrepôt of Vila Nova de Gaia, the town lying on the south bank of the River Douro opposite Oporto. They have full power to enter the shippers' premises and demand any relevant information. The Instituto keeps a tally of the movement of all wines and brandies in the shippers' lodges, particularly those of vintage and dated ports. It has large laboratories for the analysis of port and possesses an official panel of tasters to examine all ports for quality, and the high standards necessary before issuing the Certificate of Origin which, by law, must accompany each shipment. It issues a seal of guarantee for bottled ports, a numbered strip which must be attached to the neck of each bottle before shipment. In conjunction with the Casa do Douro, it establishes the minimum and maximum prices of must and grapes as well as the price of brandy annually, before the start of the vintage.

It controls the annual shipping rights which are governed by the relation between the annual shipments of each shipper and their stocks held at the end of the fiscal year, including the new wine made at the previous vintage. All wine farmers are obliged to become members of the Casa do Douro which, while defending their interests, also controls the production and circulation of wine within the Douro demarcated region. It authorises the fortification of must, it controls the entry, transit, and application of brandies destined for this fortification. It sets out annually the authorised production of must, verifies the farmers' declarations, and certifies the results. It opens and maintains a detailed account for all those in possession of musts, wines and brandies, recording in that account all the operations which result in the movement of produce, verifying the accounts and checking the operation to which they refer. No farmer or vineyard owner is authorised to plant new vineyards or even replant old ones without the permission of the Casa do Douro. This establishment is situated in the town of Regua, the official capital of the port region.

The Gremio dos Exportadores do Vinho do Porto is the legal guardian and representative association of the port shippers, all of whom must become members. It can recommend such matters as minimum prices for export, negotiate foreign trade exchanges with other products and, on behalf of the trade, deal with the subject and distribution of export quotas whenever called upon to do so. It is fully responsible to the Instituto do Vinho do Porto in all matters pertaining to maturing, stocking, blending and shipping of port in Vila Nova de Gaia. All these controls combine to ensure that port is the genuine product of the official demarcated Douro region, having been stored and matured in the sole legitimate and official entrepôt of Vila Nova de Gaia.

2

The Douro

～～✦～～

The river and the country

Rising in the snow-capped peaks of the Sierra de Urbion in Spain, this 'river of gold' crosses the Iberian Peninsula and eventually flows into the Atlantic Ocean at the city of Oporto in the north of Portugal. In Spain it is called the Duero; in Portugal, the Douro; the meaning is the same—gold. In fact, this mineral exists in the alluvial deposits of the river, though in very small quantities. And what more fitting a name could be given to a river which flows through the only region in the world where genuine port is produced?

The country is hard in every sense of the word—mountainous, arid, freezing in winter and a furnace in summer. The scattered towns and villages are few and far between. The peasants are hospitable and kindly by nature on the one hand and tough and obdurate on the other, as well they have to be to be able to survive the rigours of the climate and contend with the geographical hardships which are their lot. Through many generations they have been steeped in their particular product —wine.

The following true narrative may give you some idea of the changing vistas of the Douro in Portugal from the Spanish frontier to the Atlantic.

Sailing down the Duoro, 1953

In April 1953, the author, his wife and Robin Reid, from the

House of Croft, joined forces with John Smithes and Felix Vigne from Cockburns, and their respective wives, to emulate the voyage of the age-old Douro boats—*barcos rabelos*—which used to transport the wine down this river from the vineyards to Vila Nova de Gaia, where it is matured until it is shipped.

We could not find any historical evidence in Oporto that anyone from the British community had ever embarked on a similar expedition before, and so we considered this a worthwhile voyage to discover the trials and tribulations the boatmen of these large and historic boats underwent. The actual history of the *barco rabelo* will be told in a later chapter. We chose the month of April because it is the month that most of the wines made in the previous year come down from the Douro district, when the level of the river is high and the currents strong after a winter of heavy rain, as well as the melting snows from the high mountains in Spain. The larger boats, laden with thirty to forty pipes of port, were then able to navigate the treacherous rapids and whirlpools in the Upper Douro region.

Our captain or *mestre*, Manuel Guedes da Silva, and his crew of two boatmen, met us at the station of Pocinho near the Spanish frontier. The clouds were racing across the skies and we were informed that the weather forecast was not promising. However, armed with victuals and port, we boarded his craft, a smaller version of the *barco rabelo*, and set course for Oporto in the afternoon. Because of the uncertain weather forecast, our ex-wartime RAF navigator, John Smithes, considered that a 'log' should be written up, which he did on the side of a case of port. This, happily, is still in existence, and contains an accurate hourly record of this unique and historic experience.

Probably owing to the inclement weather there seemed to be a considerable quantity of 'rum rations' (for 'rum' read 'port') issued during the voyage, and what with numerous landings to take on provisions and wines from friendly farmers, the trip possibly took a little longer than expected. It may be recorded that these provisions included succulent roast *cabritos* (kids), suckling pigs, *bacalhau* (dried codfish), locally grown oranges and other delectable produce.

Leaving the Quinta do Vesuvio, belonging to the House of Ferreirinha, lying on the south bank of the river, stretching up from the riverside to the top of the mountain, laden with olive trees besides producing possibly one of the largest crops of port in the Douro—some 800 pipes—we approached Taylor's Quinta das Vargelas with its beautiful man-made terraces clinging to the mountain side. Opposite, on the north bank of the river, stands the Quinta dos Canais, owned by a Spanish doctor. Here many famous partridge shoots have been held, and the guns will always remember the sheer cliff-side called appropriately, Judas, where the partridge feel that no gun can get near them. The Gafaria, a well-known landmark, is in fact a solid pinnacle of schistous rock standing out like a sugarloaf sticking up into the sky. This is the home of the fox and the eagle. Anyone suffering from vertigo stays well clear of these two spots.

When shooting the dangerous and famous Cachão rapids situated below the Gafaria, the story of Baron Forrester's death there in 1846, over one hundred years previously, was brought back to us very vividly. One can well imagine how any wine boat could founder and be overturned by the sheer force of the currents and whirlpools which had to be so skilfully navigated. What admiration we all had for the boatmen, wielding their huge tiller to bring us to the comparative calm and safety of the river beyond the rapids.

Unless one has seen a whirlpool at close quarters, it would seem an impossible phenomenon. Leaning over the edge of the boat, one looked into a bottomless pit of swirling water. Such force and intensity of movement would be difficult to imagine. While we were looking into one such whirlpool, the calm voice of one of the boatmen told us how in bad weather a friend of his had fallen overboard and was unlucky enough to be sucked into the whirlpool. He graphically described his comrade's last moments and ended up by saying that only the top of his head was visible before he was finally sucked under and disappeared. Happily we did not overturn or sink, nor were we encumbered with leather belts laden with gold pieces. Had we foundered, the ladies were not wearing crinolines, which saved the

Baron's guests at that time, but could doubtless have swum more strongly than his fair ladies.

The awe-inspiring and rugged scenery around us, the schistous rocks, the sheer mountains stopping abruptly at the river's edge, the terraces of port vines clinging to their sides and, apart from a few olive groves, not a tree in sight, made us think of it as 'The Cruel Land'.

Tucked high up in the mountains was the village of Ribalonga, lying above Cockburn's Quinta do Tua on the north bank. This 'family village' was virtually run by the Carvalho family, the head of which, Antonio, died some years ago. He had brought up a family of boys who are now doctors, agronomists and engineers who sadly no longer live in the village. The inhabitants were all farmers and were proud of their port, 98 per cent of which has been sold to Croft for over eighty years. The Douro farmer is conservative in his ideas, proud in his wines and loyal to his shipper.

As we proceeded down the river in our small *rabelo* boat, we were continually greeted from the shore by the friendly inhabitants, as well as some shippers and competitors who were there visiting their *quintas* and who knew of our expedition. For instance, at Graham's Quinta Malvedos, at Tua, a salvo of rockets greeted us as we passed and messages of goodwill (and ruderies) were exchanged through megaphones.

We selected our first camping-site as dusk fell; an attractive narrow sandy beach, a cove with sheer cliffs of rock on both sides and a silver thread of water gently pouring down the chasm behind us. The boatmen rapidly lit a camp-fire of kindling wood that was strewn about and, as many had done in days gone by, we then had an excellent hot meal with plenty of wine to wash it down, ending with port which made us feel warm and contented. This proved to be a good thing, as at that moment the heavens opened and a downpour of rain began. We rapidly dispersed to our tents and slept well until dawn. An early rise next morning and oh, how spoiled we were by the kindly boatmen who had prepared us all a splendid breakfast! And thus we re-embarked and went on our way.

Continuing downriver, we passed the Robertson Brothers' Quinta do Roncão, tucked into the corner of the 'V' of the river. Here the vineyards are scattered and terraced wherever the steep mountains allow them to be planted. The wine is famous for its quality and, whenever a vintage is declared, this wine will always be included in the final blend. Reaching Croft's Quinta da Roêda at Pinhão, the surrounding mountains became less barren and rugged, and some cork trees and eucalyptus appeared, as well as orange and lemon groves. It is interesting to note that the orange tree in January and February in the Douro bears the flower, the green unripe orange and the fully ripe and sweet orange all at the same time.

Quinta das Carvalhas, owned by Companhia Vinicola, lying on the south bank opposite Roêda, prides itself in its 'mushroom'—a round building situated right on top of the mountain with magnificent panoramic views of the whole of the Alto Douro. It has all modern comforts, including an excellent round cellar of old vintage ports and table wines. Certainly a place to visit as the thirsty visitor will be well rewarded with the vistas and good wine!

Looking up the small Pinhão tributary from the Douro river, one sees the beautifully maintained Quinta do Noval with its immaculate terracing towering over the winding roads leading to Alijó, the nearest town from Pinhão, some 45 kilometres inland. And at the mouth of this small tributary, on the north bank, to the west and east one sees well-known shippers' vineyards—Warre's Quinta do Bonfim, Gonzalez Byass's Quinta da Sabordella, Calem's Quinta da Foz, Hunt Roope's Quinta da Eira Velha, and many others. This district around Pinhão is recognised as possibly, the best for port. There are many *quintas* which are situated away from the banks of the river, a little further down from Pinhão, and should you descend several gradients, you would find, nestled in the mountains, Ramos Pinto's great Quinta do Bom Retiro.

About 20 kilometres further down the river we approached Regua, the capital city of the port wine district, the mountains becoming less steep and the vineyards more plentiful, undulating and lush. Here the production is far higher than in the barren Upper Douro, due to the quality of the soil, which has more earth and less schistous rock in the valleys. Undoubtedly the quality vineyards, few and far between, lie east of Regua where the country is more barren and the schistous soil more abundant. It is strange that the difference of the countryside is so marked within such a short distance.

Leaving the official demarcated port wine district at Barqueiros, we reached Portuzelo. Here, in this granite rock valley, some tricky rowing and steering were necessary, as whirlpools and rapids were prevalent and more dangerous and in evidence following the recent rainfall and semi-flooding of the river. At this point and in similar parts of the River Douro, where it becomes narrower and the currents stronger, one could not possibly row or sail the boat upriver without the aid of footpaths or footholds, which are in fact cut out of the rocky walls on the banks to enable the boatmen to haul the boats over some of the rapids and currents by hand and rope. Sometimes, where possible, oxen were used, and at certain points there were always teams of these waiting to help the crews. But we were sailing downriver with the rain beating down on us as we sheltered under tarpaulins, singing songs and in high spirits. What a fascinating trip this was proving to be!

Our second night was spent halfway up a wooded river boundary on a verdant platform cut out by Nature to suit us—or so we thought. Again, wonderful food and a good night's sleep in our tents. It was actually fine the next morning and we set off at a rapid pace as the river was running very fast at that point and there were rapids to be negotiated. In the midst of these, a Croft wife tremulously and unhappily murmured that she had left her handbag at the camping site—murder might well have been committed at this point (by her husband) had not the captain, with great understanding, rapidly put two men and a rope ashore and bade them haul the boat back up again. This they did, singing cheerfully and with good humour, while a rapid port ration was doled out to the seething husband to keep him quiet and help abate his fury. The all-important handbag was retrieved and peace reigned once more. What better proof that port can be drunk at any time of day and in all circumstances?

As we sailed down the river, lemon and orange groves, heavily laden with fruit, stretched down to the water's edge, and the vines began to change in character. While in the Douro district, these are short and stubby, grown in regimented rows and wired, here they sprawl everywhere to a great height and are even trained up trees. The grapes produced from these vines give us the red and white *vinhos verdes*, or 'green wines', of the north of Portugal.

Leaving these vines behind us, we approached civilisation once again—our third day. We reached Entre-os-Rios, a place famous for its lampreys, those succulent eel-like fish, a surfeit of which caused the death of Henry III. We avoided catching any, as we felt they would not be good travelling companions. On towards Oporto: green banks and large houses with their gardens running down to the river, urban highways and all too soon our destination. We looked around our boat, our shabby old-fashioned tents, the Primus for cooking lunch on board, a small store of dry wood left over from our camp fires at night, nice, simple old enamelled mugs and plates, a real cast-iron 'witch of Endor' cauldron that had been used to cook our superb peasant soups each night by the captain and his loyal crew, shabbily but suitably dressed for their arduous trip. What a wonderful comradeship we had built up in our three days of travelling! How almost resentful we felt of our reception committee, who seemed to bring us back to the twentieth century with a jolt!

We all agreed that we had seen the River Douro as few, apart from the boatmen, had ever done. It was the end of a unique experience which we all felt had deepened our understanding of the Douro dwellers and indeed, the river itself. Sadly, at the time of writing, a similar trip will never again be possible because of the construction of a series of dams and locks on this river. Two have already been completed in Carrapatelo and Regua, one is under construction at Valeira, and there is a project to build two more at Crestuma and Pocinho. It will, however, be possible to navigate the changed face of the River Douro again when these are completed, and it is hoped to use 1,500-ton barges to transport wine and iron ore to Oporto.

Our trip down the river had given us a unique view of the countryside in which port is grown, and through which it passes on its way to the lodges at Vila Nova de Gaia, and with luck you have been able to appreciate something of its character. But the time has now come for facts and figures.

The quintas

To return to specific facts, the official demarcated area of the Douro district covers 242,712 hectares of land, of which only about 10 per cent is actually planted with vines at the time of writing. The remaining territory, where physically possible, is planted with almonds, olive trees, apples and citrus fruits.

Traditionally the region is divided into three parts, known as the Baixo Corgo, Cima Corgo and Douro Superior. The first zone, the Baixo Corgo, stretches on the north bank of the river Douro from Barqueiros to Vila Seca de Poiares, continuing through Canelas until it reaches the mouth of the tributary Corgo at Abaças. On the south bank it starts at Barró, finishing at the mouth of another tributary, Temi-Lobos. The second area, the Cima Corgo, stretches between the aforementioned area and the Cachão, thus leaving the third, the Douro Superior, to lie between this and the Spanish frontier. It is extremely difficult to define the borders of these three areas, simply because they are so complex on account of the mountain ranges, their altitude and geographical position, and finally, the soil.

Of the Baixo Corgo zone 28·8 per cent is planted with vines, 9·7 per cent in the Cima Corgo and only 3·0 per cent in the Douro Superior. The total production of wine in the demarcated region is approximately 200,000 pipes or 110 million litres, and this wine is produced from a total of 85,000 vineyards, which belong to roughly some 25,000 farmers, about 19,000 of whom produce five or fewer pipes of wine each per annum.

Thus approximately, the average production per hectare should be 8·2 pipes or 4,510 litres. However, it is not as easy as all this because once we start classifying the production in each *quinta* per one thousand vines in the three districts, we must forget the generally acknowledged hectare measure, and stick to the production per one thousand vines throughout. The following percentages in relation to production to farmers will give the reader a good insight to the method of growing in this region:

74% produce	1–5	pipes per annum
12% produce	6–10	pipes per annum
9% produce	11–25	pipes per annum
3% produce	26–50	pipes per annum
1·4 % produce	51–100	pipes per annum
0·6 % produce	101 or more	pipes per annum

The production of the following well-known *quintas* will give some idea of their size and relative quality.

Quinta das Carvalhas, situated on the south bank of the river and owned by the Companhia Vinicola or to give it its full name, Companhia Geral de Agricultura das Vinhas do Alto Douro, is one of the largest *quintas* in the Cima Corgo, producing between 650 and 670 pipes of wine. Approaching the town of Pinhão from the west the first thing that will be seen is this huge mountain with the terraces clinging to its side and reaching up the river for some distance. Opposite, on the north bank, tucked away at the mouth of the tributary Pinhão, lies Calem's Quinta da Foz, producing around 130 pipes.

Following the single-line railway a short distance away we come across Gonzalez Byass's Quinta da Sabordela, Warre's Quinta do Bonfim producing between 85 and 90 pipes, lying alongside Croft's Quinta da Roêda. The vines here, producing some 220 pipes, sweep round the 'V' of the river, eventually joining up with Snr Edmundo Ferreira's Quinta do Roncão of 110 pipes. The famous Quinta do Noval owned by the Van Zeller family, producing 220 pipes, lies on the west side of the mountain high above the Pinhão valley, and the whitewashed terraces can be seen for miles around.

Leaving the road running alongside the river on the south bank on the way to Regua, high on the mountainside facing north we come across the Quinta da Corte belonging to Pacheco Irmão Lda. While this *quinta* produces 200 pipes of first-class wine, there are numerous small ones dotted around producing 5 pipes or less. Nearer Regua, Barros Almeida have their Quinta de S. Luiz overlooking the river, with 150 pipes, and possibly one of the largest *quintas* in the Baixo Corgo is the Quinta do Valado belonging to Jorge Viterbo Ferreira, producing some 450–500 pipes. We have only touched on a very few *quintas* in the 0·6 per cent class, as it would need a complete book to go through the enormous list of vineyards situated in this small port district.

Before we go any further, the word *quinta* should be explained. Generally it means a farm, and this could be a fruit farm, crops, potatoes, wine or whatever. When we talk about it in this book it refers only to a vineyard. Normally, this contains the owner's house or bungalow, the workmen's living and sleeping quarters, the offices in various degrees of size, the crushing and fermenting plants, the storage lodges or *caves*, and of course the vines. But in the vineyards we also find olive trees, almonds and citrus fruit groves. Generally the bailiff and his family have their own house in the *quinta*, but the administrator usually lives either in his own or in the local town. The permanent personnel number only a few, depending upon the size of the *quinta*, as the pickers, pruners, grafters etc., only turn up at the appropriate time of the viticultural year.

For some who live in the Douro, it does not seem a colourful district, but then one remembers the mimosa in January and February, the oleanders during the summer, the heathers, the green vineyards and finally, the artist's paradise of colour when the leaves of the many varied qualities of vines turn from green into the most vivid yellows, reds and purples after the vintage. Only the lucky people who have seen this sight believe it is true.

The buildings are constructed to combat the heat of the summer. The walls are made of solid granite, sometimes a metre thick, the windows heavily shuttered to keep out the intense heat—cool in summer and cold in winter, except when open fires are available. Now that electricity is generally distributed in most parts of the Douro one does find occasionally central heating and fires. Possibly the most beautiful sights in the *quintas*, especially when they are old, are the beautiful houses, which are tiled both inside and outside, as are the *lagars* or treading tanks. Calem's Quinta da Foz, Hunt Roope's Quinta Eira Velha and Ramos Pinto's Quinta do Bom Retiro are splendid examples of this typical blue tiling. Even the railway stations on the single-track line, weaving its way from Oporto to the Spanish frontier, pride themselves on this art.

When a certain English lady from the home country remarked, on her way up the Douro to the vineyards, that all the stations were named the same, i.e. 'Senhores' and 'Senhoras', what she had seen was that even the indication of the necessities of life were in the traditional blue and white tiles!

Classification of vineyards

One of the major problems of the Casa do Douro is the control of the qualities of the wines made in these thousands of vineyards dotted all over the region. After many years of intensive study, a system of classification by points has been established which has undoubtedly produced the desired results.

Briefly, this means that each vineyard is classified in accordance with three criteria—the soil, the climate and the agricultural conditions. The soil is, again, subdivided into the nature of the land, the composition, the production, the gradient of the vineyard, and the type of soil itself. The climate is subdivided into the position of the vineyard in relation to the demarcated region, the altitude, degree of protection from the elements, and the general layout. Finally, the agricultural conditions are subdivided into the varieties of the grapes growing in the vineyard, the age of the vines, and the general cultivation and maintenance of the particular vineyard. Each subdivision is given a maximum number of points which can add up to a total of 1,680.

		Points
(a)	Production	120
(b)	Soil	180
(c)	Gradient	100
(d)	Altitude	150
(e)	Geographical position	600
(f)	Position in relation to climatic conditions	210
(g)	Upkeep and maintenance	100
(h)	Qualities of grapes	150
(i)	Age of vines	70
	TOTAL	1,680

Once the vineyards have been awarded their respective points, they are then classified by the official team of government viticultural experts and graded from A to F. Dependent on the final grading, an official authorisation is given to the farmer to permit him to make so many litres of port per 1,000 vines:

A 1,200 or more points = 700 litres per 1,000 vines
B 1,001 or more points = 700 litres per 1,000 vines
C 801 or more points = 500 litres per 1,000 vines
D 601 or more points = 400 litres per 1,000 vines
E 401 or more points = 300 litres per 1,000 vines
F 201 or more points = No authorisation

The balance of the production in the various categories which are not authorised to be made into port is then made into table wine. The whole system is designed to ensure that the authorised production of port per annum at the vintage is of the highest quality. This is particularly important in a world where wine is becoming increasingly popular. The status of port must be maintained.

The factors mentioned in the point system are, without doubt, the principal ones which make up the ultimate quality of a vineyard. For instance, in the Upper Corgo, 1,000 vines will produce only 550 litres or less, while in the Lower Corgo the production could be anything up to 2,000 litres per 1,000 vines.

The schistous soil produces a wine of the highest quality but a small yield. The gradient of the vineyard can determine the amount of vines to be planted per acre, as in some cases the terraces will only allow two or three rows. No port is allowed to be made from vines planted higher than 500 metres above sea level. It is strange that in such a small area the local geographical position has been proved to determine the quality and the quantity of the vines and grapes.

Again, the *quintas* of the 'rising sun', facing east, will be relatively cooler than those of the 'setting sun', which suffer the broiling sun of the afternoon because the mountains of the region run from north to south. Others facing south, which are not so steep, have concentrated heat all day and produce a high quality with a relative reduction in quantity, due to the burning and shrivelling of a large proportion of the grapes.

Upkeep and maintenance is an all-important factor in vineyards and farms throughout the whole world, and it is always a sad sight to see a badly maintained vineyard with wires broken, the vines choked with weeds, and sometimes even unpruned from the previous year. The grape varieties again differ in the various parts of the district, depending upon the climate and position of the *quinta*. Some of the best varieties do not grow so well in the Lower Corgo as they do in the Upper Corgo and similarly, some varieties give a very much greater yield but produce lower-quality wine. The age of the vine comes into the point system at this stage, as the older the vine the better the quality, but naturally, the lower the yield per vine. Normally the vines should be uprooted and replaced by new ones every thirty to forty years. All these factors lead up to the final authorisation of the quantity of port to be made at the vintage of any one year.

By law, a shipper may only export approximately one-third of his stocks annually. With accurate forecasting, the port shipper knows how much he needs to make at the vintage, and he advises the Instituto do Vinho do Porto of this quantity. The Instituto then collates these quantities from every shipper and agrees with the Casa do Douro the total amount of port that should be made in that year. An official government bulletin is issued in the national press, usually in August, confirming the total authorised quantity of port to be made at that vintage as well as the minimum prices of must and brandy. For example, the figure for 1972 was 80,000 pipes, and the total production of wine in the Douro district was 220,000 pipes; therefore, the balance of 140,000 pipes was made into table wine and the 80,000 pipes of port were allocated among the 25,000 farmers apportioned on the point system. This also guarantees that the best grapes are chosen from every vineyard for the production of port.

Soil and climate

The distinctive qualities of port are only in part attributable to the method of its production; to the geological and climatic conditions in which the vines are grown are the unchangeable factors that ultimately control the style of the wine. The volcanic soil of the Douro region is impregnated with a soft, foliated stone, rich in phosphates, known as schist. It is from this soil that much of the wine's uniqueness is derived. It is rich in potassium and magnesium, poor in nitrogen and organic substances, and totally lacking in lime. It must have been thrown up by some gigantic volcanic eruption as, below the schistous stratum, there lies an iron-hard stratum of black volcanic rock and large masses of granite which appear on the surface here and there throughout the region.

The country is precipitous and the vines are grown on walled terraces made from the schistous rock, cut into the hillside to ensure that the heavy rains, when they fall, do not uproot and sweep away the vines. These rains, which fall heavily between November and March, percolate through the schistous rock until they reach the non-porous layer, thus creating deep reserves of moisture from which the vines feed during the dry periods between April and October, when the rains virtually cease apart from the occasional heavy thunderstorm. The soil in the Douro district can be assessed according to the content of schist: the higher the percentage, the lower the yield and the higher the quality. There is, in fact, a very distinctive physical division of soil, and one finds the further east one travels upriver to the Spanish frontier, the heavier the concentration of this soil. There is no doubt that nowhere in the wine-producing areas of the world is there a more difficult and more expensive land to

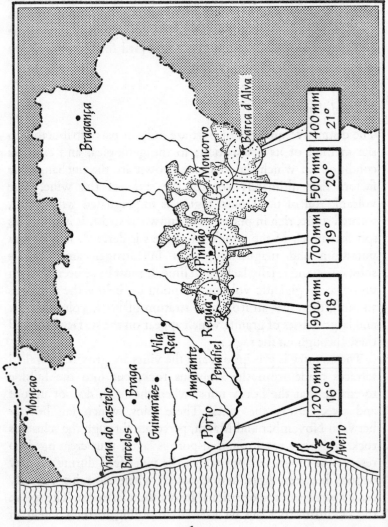

cultivate than the Douro district, and possibly less wine is produced per vine, on average, than in any others, resulting in a very high cost of production. The Douro climate is greatly influenced by the range of mountains of which the backbone is formed by the Serra do Marão, with peaks reaching to over 1,200 m. This mountain range seals off the Douro wine-growing region from the north and west and, catching much of the rain, creates a considerable variance in rainfall between the wine-growing district and the coast. For instance, the average annual rainfall in Oporto is 1,200 mm, while only 400 mm fall at Barca d'Alva, the most eastern point of this region, on the Portuguese-Spanish frontier. These mountains also protect the vineyards from a certain amount of frost and strong winds, though heavy hailstones and violent thunderstorms are not uncommon, even up to the end of the month of August. It is devastating to see the results of a twenty-minute hailstorm having cut through a vineyard like a sharp knife, leaving complete destruction in that very short time and causing a loss of thousands of litres of wine to the farmer.

Strangely, this area itself contains a considerable number of microclimates, particularly in the upper regions of the Douro. These are largely created by the aspects of the valleys and the protection afforded by the surrounding hills. This accounts, in a large measure, for the number of different styles of port produced in the region.

It will be interesting to see the possible effects on the future climate of this region resulting from the large masses of water which will be built up behind the dams now under construction. Water is a good absorbent of heat and, at the same time, gives off a considerable quantity of cooling vapour. Therefore, it is a more efficient regulator of climate than the soil. In large dams, the water is cooler than the surrounding soil during the day and at night the effect is the opposite. It is possible that with the construction of these dams down the river the climate could become relatively cooler, and it is anticipated that the quality of wine produced in the vineyards near the dams will become even higher than at present. For example, since the canalisation of the

River Moselle, it has been generally accepted that the wines grown there are better even than before.

Prayers are offered by the farmers for rain during the winter months and early spring so that the reserves may be built up to withstand the tremendous heat in the summer. The average rainfall in the Douro region ranges between 900 mm at Regua and 400 mm at Barca d'Alva, while the average annual temperature is officially recorded as being between 18° and 21°C, but these figures tend to be misleading as there can be a vast variation in temperature from below 0°C in the winter to as high as 45°C in the summer. Snow is seldom seen but the east winds blowing from Spain have a drastic effect on the cultivation, as they are not only freezing but intensely dry in winter, and boiling hot and just as dry in summer. This gives one some idea of what the farmers have to contend with climatically.

Co-operative policies

The Portuguese government in the last twenty-five years has encouraged the establishment of wine co-operatives all over the country owing to the difficulty experienced by the small wine farmers in economically and efficiently producing and marketing their wines. These co-operatives cover all the wine-growing areas and have been built with government loans at low interest rates.

The local smallholders become partners in the operation by handing in their grapes at the vintage time to these centres, where they are given a credit card for the weight of the grapes supplied. The government has also taken steps during the last few years to assist these co-operatives in marketing their wines. They are, generally speaking, well operated, with good technicians and responsible and qualified directors. This is particularly evident in the Vinho Verde district in the north of Portugal in the Minho, which has been formed into what can be described as a demarcated wine-producing region where strict control of quality, production and brands are practised. The same principles apply in the valley of Dão, where no bottled wines can be sold until they reach the age of 18 months. Another district where this procedure has been most marked is the area north-west of Vila Real and stretching to the Spanish frontier.

Most of the co-operatives in Portugal have limited themselves to sales in casks to the big wine-exporting companies or to selling their wine locally in 5-litre demijohns and branded bottles to small taverns and grocers. However, it has been noted in the trade press that one or two groups of co-operatives have started exporting direct to the various markets of the world using their own brands, such as Vercoop, Cartaxo, Chaves and others.

At the time of writing, exports of Portuguese table wines are still almost completely in the hands of a few companies such as *Sogrape, Gonçalvinhos, Borges, Casalinho* and *Real Vinicola* in the north and *José Maria da Fonseca, J. Serra* and a few others in the south. In the Douro district, however, the position is rather different, owing to the fact that two completely different kinds of wines, port and table wines, are produced there. Originally co-operatives in this area were destined only for the vinification of the surplus wine grown in the region after the official authorisation of the quantity of port to be made at that vintage was produced, and they were then forbidden to produce port.

However, in the last few years, some have succeeded in obtaining official permission to make port and such centres as Regua, Freixo, Moncorvo and Alijó have been doing so and offering it to the shippers. Undoubtedly they will grow in number owing to the large numbers of small farmers, but the shippers, who are also increasing their production centres and vineyards, will, we trust, continue to have the final word in the style and quality of the port wine of their House.

3

The Vine

Classification of grapes and vines

Prior to the attack of the *phylloxera* pest, which we shall deal
with in more detail later on in this chapter, vines were produced
from the root-stocks that were native to the Douro and some of
which could well have dated from pre-Roman times. Many of
the great vine stocks of Europe, which probably originated in
that era, have been planted in every corner of the globe and,
naturally enough, have become so well acclimatised as to appear
indigenous to the soil and climate of their particular area. Thus
the resultant vines have their completely individual character
and in this way the characteristics of the various vineyards of the
world have come about. However, most of the vines used in the
Douro region are undoubtedly of French origin and it would
seem that the strains which continue to be most widely planted
are descended from the Pinot varieties.

In the seventeenth century, a sporting Scot by the name of
Robert Archibald acquired the Quinta de Roriz as a shooting-
lodge, having discovered that the redleg partridge, the wolf and
the wild boar were abundant there. Naturally wishing a return
on his investment, he thought that there could be a possibility
of growing vines in this area because of the natural surroundings
and climate. He sent his son to Burgundy to obtain a large
quantity of vine cuttings of a red grape—the Pinot Noir—which
formerly Count Henry of Burgundy brought over to Guimaraens in 1095. This vine grew rapidly and abundantly and he was
thus able to produce his own red, heavy table wines. This variety

of grape has become most popular in the Douro region, and to-day it is called the *Tinta Francisca* or *Tinta Francesca*.

More than forty different varieties of vines are planted in the Douro district, twenty-eight of which are red and nineteen white. The question is often asked why it is necessary to have so many varieties to produce port, especially as in Jerez there are only three main varieties used to make sherry and in Bordeaux only half a dozen to make both red and white Bordeaux. The answer is the way in which, in the Douro region, the various vines and grapes react to the soils and microclimates, though in the larger vineyards one finds anything up to thirteen or fourteen varieties used to produce the particular style of port required.

The varieties are sometimes extreme: for instance the Sousão grape has a tremendous amount of colour—even the juice is red—but has little natural sweetness, and is prolific in the Lower Corgo area although it is not generally grown in the Upper Corgo, where the soil and climate do not suit it. On the other hand, the Rufete, a very sweet and highly aromatic grape, has little colour and a very small yield and is normally seen in the Upper Corgo. There is also the Malvasia Preta, a superior variety which only grows in the area between Tua and Roncão. This is a very sweet grape and produces a large yield. Another abundant producer is the Touriga, which matures early and often has as many as three bunches on the same stalk. The Tinta Francisca, which we have already mentioned, produces round, very dark, violet-tinted grapes which easily come off their stalks, and are succulent and very juicy. They have a thick skin, while the Tinta Carvalha has a thin skin and is rather insipid.

This may help to explain the great differences there are in the various types and styles of vines in the Douro which, blended together and grown in their most favourable areas, produce the desired results. The official classification of these grapes is as follows:

RED	WHITE
Very good	*Very good*
Bastardo	Donzelinho
Donzelinho Tinto	Esgana-Cão
Mourisco	Folgosão
Touriga Francesa	Gouveio or Verdelho
Tinta Roriz	Malvasia Fina
Tinta Francisca	Malvasia Rei
Tinto Cão	Rabigato
Touriga Nacional	Viosinho
Good	*Good*
Cornifesto	Arinto
Malvasia Preta	Boal
Mourisco de Semente	Cercial
Periquita	Codega
Rufete	Malvasia Corada
Samarrinho	Moscatel Galego
Sousão	
Tinta Amarela	
Tinta da Barca	
Tinta Barroca	
Tinta Carvalha	
Touriga Brasileira	
Average	*Average*
Alvarelhão	Branco sem Nome
Avesso	Fernão Pires
Casculho	Malvasia Parda
Castela	Pedernão
Coucieira	Praça
Moreto	Touriga Branca
Tinta Bairrada	
Tinto Martins	

The big problem for the local farmer in a low-yield vine-growing region such as the Douro is to find a balance between quality and production. The temptation to plant a higher-yield vine, and thus lower quality, is almost irresistible as high quality is synonymous with a low yield. Fortunately the classification of vineyards mentioned in Chapter II deals with this problem very effectively.

To summarise the forty-eight above-mentioned varieties, some of the older works on the subject of port mention such strains as Bastardo, Alvarelhão and Donzelinho as being of top quality. Today, however, it would be more correct to say that those varieties most in use are Mourisco, Tinta (Francisca, Amarela, Tinto Cão) and Tourigas, which are best known for their quality in the *quintas* of the Upper Corgo. The Mourisco vines are very healthy and produce an excellent quality. The grapes are generally large in size, but the colour is not a strong point in this particular strain. Generally the skin is fairly thin and the grapes on each bunch ripen unevenly.

The Tinta family, however, are perhaps the finest grown in the Douro valley, particularly the Francisca and the Amarela. This variety bears up extremely well and is very resistant to fungoid diseases such as oidium (described later). The Amarela is easily distinguishable by the stem, which is light brown in colour, and the bunches of all the Tintas are fairly large (with the exception of the Tinto Cão) and tend to be compact and very dark in colour. This grape is very resistant to damp conditions and does not suffer much from *coulure*, to which the Mouriscos are very subject. *Coulure*, or *Clorose*, is not a disease but purely a condition of the vine which has reacted to soil and weather conditions. It can easily be picked out in a vineyard by the leaves turning yellow. The Touriga, which again is a stout and vigorous producer, is fairly resistant to fungoid diseases due to its thick and pigmented skin and loosely formed bunches.

Perhaps one should mention at this stage the famous Roriz variety which one associates very closely with the Tintas, the great difference being that the Roriz produces possibly the highest-graded musts in the whole Douro valley. Relatively very dark black grapes, fairly hard skins and very high sugar content are the main characteristics of this variety. Lunching at Gonzalez Byass in 1953, a Roriz unfortified wine (which had an alcoholic strength of 17·5°) was offered to the author as the red wine to accompany a delicious meal of partridge. It was a beautiful and unique wine which resembled a bone-dry vintage port; but its effects reduced the consumption of the 1927 vintage port afterwards!

Formerly there was a considerable trade in fortified Muscatel, two of the best-known vine varieties being Muscatel de Hamburgo and Muscatel de Jesus. The former of the two is by far the more aromatic and attractive, with larger grapes and bunches, but the skins of both are thin, and thus liable to attacks of fungoid diseases. The main market for this type of fortified wine was Brazil and, prior to the First World War, great quantities were shipped to Russia. Unfortunately both these markets for this wine have now ceased to exist and today the vineyards which surround the small town of Alijó in the Upper Corgo, once almost exclusively planted to meet this demand, now sell their grapes to a local co-operative which produces a pleasant table wine.

The process of producing a fortified Muscatel wine differs from that used when making port from other varieties of grapes. The reason is that the aroma and taste of the Muscatel grape is largely concentrated in the skin. To preserve these, two basic methods are used. The first is to extract large quantities of the skins from the must, prior to fermentation, and to toast them in the hot sun for several days. The skins, when dry, are then put back into the wine which has been fortified with *aguardente*, thus enhancing the finished wine with the heavy, sweet scent of the grape. The second method is to extract large quantities of the skins after crushing and to soak them for several days in *aguardente*, the resultant infusion of skins and brandy then being added to the finished wine. Normally speaking, the Muscatel wines have their fermentation arrested at a very early stage in order to preserve the maximum amount of natural sugar, and these wines are nowadays almost exclusively used for blending.

Little has been said of the white varieties in the Douro district. Possibly this is due to the fact that (to quote an adage) 'Port has two duties—the first to be red and the second to be drunk.' However, white port is an essential product for blending purposes as well as a straight drink, a medium or dry apéritif, extremely popular in France, Sweden, Norway and Britain as well as in Portugal. Perhaps the best-known grapes in general use today are limited to two varieties of Malvasia, the Rei and the Fina, which produce the best white ports in the Douro.

Structure of the grape

Having described the varieties of vines and grapes in the Douro valley, as well as the climatic conditions and soil, we shall now turn to the grape itself and describe the components and functions of this extremely interesting fruit. The following cross-section of the grape is possibly the best way of illustrating this:

Stalk: this conducts the nourishment to the pip. Largely composed of water and tannin and a certain quantity of free acids.

This section contains the principal sugar content. Owing to water volume, the density is very much less than **e**. Tartaric acid, free acids and a small quantity of albumen.

Umbilical cord or navel-string.

Normally two pips and two cords attached. Sometimes some grapes have three pips. When the grape is ripe they take on a brown colour. Rich in water, oil and tannin.

The sliminess and density of the texture of this section of the grape is due to the presence of albuminoid and nitrogenous substances. There is no tartaric acid and hardly any sugar, but cream of tartar and free acids are evident.

Pulp: rich in sugar.

This section controls the tannin, colour and scent.

Skin: consists of cellulose, tannin, essential oils and colour materials—yellow for white grape, bluish-purple for red grape.

69

The pigments which colour grapes are formed in the leaves, and are transferred to the grapes themselves in colourless form as soon as they reach the right stage of ripeness. The colouring process then takes place through oxidation.

Vine diseases

It is a strange fact that virtually no diseases appeared in the Douro valley before 1850, when the oidium plague attacked the vineyards of this area. This disease came from the United States of America and was closely followed, in 1868, by the killer pest, the *phylloxera*, from the same country, which virtually destroyed all the vineyards in Europe. Mildew was first noted in the valley in 1870, and we shall deal with this disease first as it is the most severe problem today.

Mildew is provoked by the fungus *Plasmopora viticola*, which develops in the green parts of the vine, affecting the branch, leaves, flowers and the fruit itself. When this mildew appears on the leaves, it takes the form of darkish transparent spots which slowly become white and look like mould. Unless treated, the leaves will eventually dry and fall from the vines. This, of course, is a most serious matter as the sugar which eventually reaches the grapes is first formed in the leaves; they are virtually the lungs of the vine and the perfect sunshade during the heat of the day.

This fungus attacks by penetrating the cells of the vine, attacking the young shoots and embryo bunches. When this occurs, these bunches never develop. If the attack comes at a later date, when the bunches are formed and maturing, the disease can easily be recognised by the fact that the grapes develop grey or blue spots, eventually turning brown and then shrinking and shrivelling in the hot sun. The climatic conditions have a very important effect on mildew, which tends to grow at a fairly high temperature, after a long spell of sun, when rain is heavy and the humidity is high.

Various products are used to combat this disease, such as copper sulphate, copper oxides, organic compounds, fungicides (zineb and captan), as well as mixtures of fungicides with a copper base.

Oidium is another most destructive disease, caused by the fungus *Uncinula necator*. In the mid-nineteenth century it attacked the vines in France, Spain and Portugal and spread so rapidly that the farmers feared total destruction of their vines and foresaw ruination for themselves.

Unlike mildew, this fungus forms only on the surface of all green parts of the plant. It appears in the form of mould on the young shoots and leaves, giving them a whitish, powdery aspect. When branches are affected, they dry up and die, and the grapes harden and split. The disease can, however, be easily recognised, as the branches of the vine show dark, shadowy spots along their entire length. This fungus can grow and develop at a lower temperature, 25°C–30°C being ideal, and like mildew, flourishes in conditions of high humidity.

Flowers of sulphur is the best product to use against oidium, not only in powder form but also incorporated in cupric mixtures. Normally, purified sulphur, flowers of sulphur and granulated sulphur are used in the powder treatments, while wet sulphur, micro-sulphur and colloidal sulphur are incorporated in cupric and other mixtures. Fortunately the value of sulphur in combating the disease was discovered in the earliest days, as soon as it struck. However, if these preventive treatments are either not used or the gods are against the farmer, potassium permanganate may be used in severe cases as a powerful cure. It acts as a strong oxidising agent and destroys the fungus immediately. Although this cure is rapid, it is not a preventive treatment and it is advisable to use sulphur after a dose of potassium.

These are really the only two important diseases caused by fungi, but, unhappily, through these two diseases, another fungus rears its ugly head, and this only attacks the bunches once they have developed. There is no sign of infection until it has taken a firm hold of the grape itself, and by that time it is incurable. This is called the *Podridão dos Cachos* (*Botrytis cinerea*), also known as grey rot when it attacks the young fruit and brown rot when it infects the riper fruit.

This form of rot attacks bunches which have been hit by hail-stones and therefore have broken skins. It normally attacks regions already infected by other parasites and is easily recognisable, as the grapes grow dark purple and a flowery rot is formed over their entire surface. Humidity is again the enemy which causes this fungus to grow, typically after rain following a hot spell. *Botrytis cinerea* resists the anti-cupric cryptogamic products usually used, and the cupric products, which are usually so effective in combating mildew, have much less effect on this kind of rot. Although it is advisable to use cupric-aluminium mixtures or powderings, which include quicklime and aluminium sulphate, these products are not altogether reliable. In fact, in this case, prevention is certainly better than cure, as there seems to be no cure!

A less common disease, known internationally as *Rougeot* (*Pseudopeziza tracheiphila*) generally attacks the vines at the end of May or the middle of June. The leaves show yellow spots which are limited in area by the actual veins of the leaf itself. The white grape leaf, when attacked, grows brown spots with yellow edges, and the red grape leaf develops purple spots with green edges. Where the vines have been infected by this disease, the leaves often shed in August and September, leaving the vines bare.

Anthracnose, provoked by the fungus *Gloeosporium ampelophagum*, is seldom seen in the Douro valley, as it requires a high humidity and can only develop in vineyards situated in narrow and humid valleys. The normal preventive spraying for mildew suffices to counteract this fungus, should there be any such physical conditions as to allow it to appear.

Another disease called Maromba appeared many years ago, but it is only in the last fifteen years that the cause of this strange crinkling of the leaves has been discovered. In the old days, vines were often planted in areas where pine trees had existed and here this disease rapidly became evident. Dark brown pits appeared on the back of the leaves, which then crinkled and dried. Fortunately the cause has now been discovered: it was found that the pine trees completely lacked borax, as did the soil surrounding them. To cure this, borax is ploughed into the soil and the disease has never reappeared.

Vine pests

The main parasites which attack the vines in the Douro district are many and varied so it would therefore be better to limit this section to the ones which are most destructive. Obviously the *phylloxera* was and still remains the greatest enemy, but we shall elaborate on this parasite later and start off with the caterpillars.

Some years ago a small, almost invisible insect called the Sphynx was found gnawing at the vines and shoots, but they have now, thankfully, become very rare. During their caterpillar stage, they were very damaging indeed, later becoming butterflies which only flew in the early evening.

More dangerous are the caterpillars which gnaw the grapes: the Pyrale butterfly and the two types of grape moths, *Cochilis* and *Eudemis*. These latter lay their eggs on the flowers and bunches of the vine. In each case the resultant caterpillars destroy the flowers and eat away the contents of the grapes themselves. The bunches attacked by the grape moths are easily recognisable as cobwebs are formed between the grapes. The Pyrale (*Sparganothis pilleriana*) is a butterfly which lays its eggs on the leaves of the vines. It then attacks the young shoots and creates a white web round the leaves and young shoots to provide itself with some protection. These caterpillars are very active and survive the winter months and the intense cold of the Douro valley by penetrating deep into the bark of the vines.

There are also two types of red spider, the *Paratetranychus pilosus* and the *Tetranychus urticae-althaeae*. The first lays its eggs on the bark of the vine; these usually hatch shortly before the vines shoot in early spring. This spider attacks the young shoots and leaves, which it destroys, causing serious damage to the crop. The second is less common and normally attacks the surrounding vegetation before passing on to the vines, which it then proceeds to destroy.

Another parasite, a small beetle which can be either green or brown, is known in the Douro as the *Charuteiro* (*Byctiscus betulae*). The female lays her eggs, usually in the centre of the leaf, which then shrivels and forms itself into a cocoon round the main stem of the leaf. The vines then take on a strange look as if they have several brown cigar-shapes hanging from them (*charuto* means cigar, hence the name given to this parasite).

A further destructive beetle known as the *Gorgulho da Videira* (*Otiorrhyncus sulcatus*) attacks the young buds, causing particular damage to the young vines. It lays its eggs in the crevices in the bark of the vine, and the resulting larvae attack both the vines and roots. Any treatment used to kill this pest must therefore involve the treatment of the soil as well as the vine. Today modern insecticides are used very satisfactorily, and should such pests appear they can be quickly and thoroughly dealt with by the farmer.

Phylloxera

One of the greatest disasters to strike the vine in Europe came to light in London where, in 1863 a sample of insects discovered on a vine in a wealthy businessman's greenhouse in Hammersmith was sent to Professor West, the famous botanist and entomologist at Oxford University. Only five years later, however, was the insect identified as and named *phylloxera*. Pasteur found that this louse originated from vines imported from North America.

In the same year as the Hammersmith incident, there was an alarming rumour in France of an 'unknown disease' which was attacking the vineyards lying on the slopes of the Bas-Rhône; by 1867 it had spread to such an extent that the farmers were extremely troubled. What alarmed the farmers mostly was that there appeared to be no cause for the new disease.

In 1866 the wine growers in Saint Martin-de-Crau had noticed a number of vines whose leaves had lost their normal green colour and which were turning yellow, with their edges becoming red. They then turned dark red and by the end of August every one of them had shrivelled and fallen. At the beginning of December, during the pruning season, most of the affected vines were dry and brittle, and some were dead. Where there were grapes during the vintage, they were acid and watery, the black grapes remaining red or pink, producing very poor wine with no bouquet, with little colour and unpleasant on the palate. Where the bunches were large, these just dried up and fell off the branches. This development in some cases took up to three years, depending upon the strength and size of the vine and its roots, but in the third year all the vines were dead.

This again caused some astonishment as, when the roots were dug up, they were found to be black and rotting, but no insects were found; they had already moved on to the next victim. The disease spread rapidly throughout the vineyards of Europe. Possibly the first actual attack of the louse was at Pujault, in the Gard, as early as 1863, but only in August 1868 did the Professor of Pharmacy of Montpellier University, Monsieur J. E. Planchon, name the insect *Phylloxera vastatrix*, having first given it a provisional name, *Rhizaphis*—'root aphis' from the Greek.

Although the pest first appeared in Portugal in 1868, it was only confirmed in 1871 and, strangely, it did not spread as rapidly as might have been expected. However, by 1881 the port shippers were predicting the end of the port trade; the entire production of that year amounted to some 6,000 pipes in an area planted to produce 250,000 pipes. Even today the graveyards of these fertile vineyards and terraces can be seen, as many farmers, ruined by this scourge, left the country and found a new life in other parts of the world such as Brazil. It seems tragic that these resilient people, who had withstood so many hardships inflicted upon them by the natural elements of the soil and climate, should be driven away from their vineyards by this invading parasite.

As far back as 1564 French colonists in America are said to have planted European vines in Florida, and by 1630 the British colonists had also planted them in Virginia. However, the life of these vineyards was short as they gradually dried up and died. Following the continued failure of these imported vines, a number of farmers started to grow the pest-resistant native grapes, Mr Longworth of Ohio being one of the first large producers in 1823.

It has been said that M. Gason Bazille first suggested what was to be the solution: the grafting of the European vine on to the American stock, at the Beaune Congress of 1869; but later a M. Laliman claimed that honour as he was the first to give information on the resistance to the pest of these American vines. Foëx, in fact, had already maintained that the *phylloxera* could not be a European pest because it would have wiped out the vine as a species and become extinct itself due to the lack of food. He came to the conclusion that either the American stock should be planted in France, which did not produce a very palatable wine, or the European vine should be grafted on to the American stock, and today the latter is the accepted universal method applied in all European vineyards.

Phylloxera is commonly called the plant or vine louse. Its name comes from the Greek *phyllon*, meaning 'leaf', and *xeros*, 'dry'. The pest has a life-cycle so remarkable and complex that it is not easy to find where to begin. It belongs to the Hemiptera order of insects, which includes bugs; all these are sucking insects which damage plants by sucking the sap. *Phylloxera* is an aphid. We must now quote from Mr George Ordish's *The Great Wine Blight* (Dent, 1972): his detailed description of the life-cycle of this insect on an American vine:

(1) The winter egg, usually found in a crack in the bark of two-year-old wood. In spring this hatches to (2) a fundatrix nymph, females only being produced. The nymph climbs up to the upper side of a young leaf, inserts its proboscis and sucks in sap as food. At the same time she injects a substance into the leaf which causes the cells to develop in a certain way, in fact, to form a gall, protected at the entrance with hairs (3). The nymph becomes adult and lays (4) yellow eggs in a circle inside the gall. These eggs hatch and become (5) gall-living female nymphs, which creep out past the protecting hairs, settle on the same or another leaf and start producing their own

galls. They grow into (6) gall-living adults who lay eggs in the gall in the same way as the fundatrix adult (No. 3 above). Three or four generations of gall-livers may be produced, becoming less fecund with each generation, but still alarmingly fertile. Whereas the fundatrix adult lays 500 to 600 eggs, the fourth generation female lays but 100. This means that one winter egg is potentially the forebear of 4,800 million gall-living females by midsummer, the time of the fourth generation. Among the third and fourth generation gall-living nymphs will be found some (7) migrant nymphs (all female still). These move down to the roots of the plant where they settle, suck sap and become (8) root-living adults. These settle either on (i) lateral parts of young roots, producing some deformities (*phylloxera* galls) and tending to prevent increase of root diameter, or (ii) on the point of a young root, near the cap-forming layer (the calyptrogon) where they stop its growth by the mechanical action of the mouth tube and the injection of saliva. The root-living adults lay (9) root eggs which later hatch into (10) root-living nymphs which become (8) root-living adults which lay (9) eggs. Three or four generations are passed in this way (stages 8, 9, 10). As the weather cools, some eggs (9) hatch to either stage 11 or stage 12: (11) Sexuperous nymphs (12) overwintering, or resting, root forms (rare on 'American' species). In the spring they continue the root-living cycle (8, 9, 10). On some stage (11) nymphs wing buds develop and the nymphs become (13) winged oviparous female adults which come out of the ground and find leaves either by climbing or flying short distances. These females conceive two eggs each, only one of which is laid, on the upper surface of a leaf. The eggs are either stage 14 or stage 15: (14) eggs producing males or (15) eggs producing females. The female-producing eggs are larger than the male-producing ones. In due course the eggs hatch, giving rise respectively to stages 16 and 17: (16) male nymphs and (17) female nymphs, growing to (18) male adults and (19) female adults. After mating the female descends to the two-year-old wood and lays a single (1) winter egg. The cycle is complete.

Mr Ordish continues by saying that it is most unusual for the American life-cycle to take place on the European vine (*vinifera*). Both winter eggs and leaf galls are rare and the life-cycle consists almost entirely of the parthenogenetic root-living forms repeated endlessly, with the winter passed as the resting stage.

The fundatrix nymph is clear yellow in colour when hatching from the winter egg and grows to between 0·25 mm and 0·45 mm in length after three months, when adult. The fundatrix is wingless, while the sexuperous adult has two pairs of transparent wings of a spread of about 3 mm and a body length of about 1·14 mm. It has a hideous greenish-yellow body with a broad head and large red eyes.

The root-living aphids rest in the roots during the cold weather with their feeding tubes inserted into the root tissues, and the effect on these roots depends upon the size of the roots and the species of the vine. When the root has been virtually sucked dry and the vine dies, the aphid then moves on to another. This is the reason why it took such a long time to discover the pest: when the dead vine was uprooted, no insect was to be found.

Although many attempts have been made to exterminate the *phylloxera*, none has been successful. Artificial and natural manures were used to attempt to combat the plague as well as fumigation of the roots and soil with carbon disulphide, organic acids and arsenic compounds. The first had a limited success but it was found impossible to control the pest on a large scale. It was even suggested to M. Planchon in 1890 that 'a living toad should be buried under the vine to draw the poison to it' but the idea was not received with great enthusiasm! Again, as the *phylloxera* cannot live in sandy soil, it was suggested that sand should be mixed with the various soils in Europe to prevent the spreading of the pest. However, the cost of this operation and the resultant thinner wines caused this suggestion to be shelved. Seemingly the only remedy was to dig out the dead vines, destroy them, and replant the vineyard with the American stock.

The first *quinta* in which the *phylloxera* appeared in the Douro district was the Quinta da Azinheira belonging to Snr Conselheiro Lopo Vaz de Sampaio e Mello, in Sabrosa. His production of fifty-five pipes in 1865 was reduced to one pipe by 1872.

In the Douro valley, the *Vitis rupestris*, with their thick barks, are the most popular of the American stocks used; the introduction of these in 1882 turned the tide and the feared destruction of the farmers' livelihoods did not take place. The wines made from the grafted vines were found to be lighter in colour and substance than those produced from the straight national vines, but quicker maturing.

This latter comment leads us on to a very interesting discussion held, a short while ago, with Snr Frederico Van Zeller, a director of the port shippers, Quinta do Noval—Vinhos S.A.R.L. This renowned gentleman, with fifty years' experience in the port trade, actually possesses in his *quinta* some 4,000 pre-*phylloxera* vines, which produce the unique *nacional* port. This is the product of 'national' ungrafted vines, which theoretically should be non-existent. They comprise varieties such as the Tourigas, Tinta Francisca, Roriz and others. From this small quantity of vines only an average of three pipes is produced per annum as the actual grapes are much smaller than the ones grown on the grafted vines. However, the colour is far deeper and the texture of the wine harder and much fuller than the post-*phylloxera* wines. In fact, Snr Van Zeller stated that the famous 1931 *nacional* was virtually undrinkable after twenty-five years in bottle!

When asked what type of treatment of the soil, the vines and the roots of these had been necessary over so many years, he replied that every six to eight years a kind of 'injection' of *sulfurete* (carbon disulphide) had been applied to the roots, but nothing had been done for at least twenty-five years, and the 'mortality' of these vines had been far less than the normal grafted ones. So where does this lead us? It seems reasonable to suggest that these *nacional* vines have become immune to the pest, as are the American stocks. In fact, when asked, Snr Van Zeller informed us that, when a *nacional* vine died after its natural life span, a shoot from its neighbour was planted, and this automatically took, without any treatment whatsoever.

What an extremely interesting study this could create in the future!

Many years ago, a remark from one of our elderly directors, known in the trade as 'Uncle Pickwick', brought home this difference when he was discussing the merits of the '42s. When reminded that the 1942 was a wartime vintage and rather light in colour and body owing to its late bottling in 1945, his scornful reply was '1842, my boy, not 1942!' It is a tragedy that stocks of this famous vintage no longer exist.

During the virtual annihilation of the vines in the Douro, it was natural that the Portuguese government took steps to replace the disaster by a series of experimental plantations in the district. These comprised the planting of tobacco, coffee, tea, citrus fruits and many other commodities. Tobacco and *maté* tea were fairly successful, but by the early 1890s when the grafting had been accepted, and tobacco was being imported from Africa at a much lower price, the vine and the grape resumed its natural life.

4

Viticulture in the Douro

The yearly cycle

As the gathering of grapes in September is considered the climax of the viticultural year, we shall begin the cycle of work in the vineyards after this date. By the middle of October, the bustle of this most important period is virtually over for another year, and the farmers and shippers are discussing the results of the three or four weeks' work around the clock, since the grape, when fermenting, waits for no man. How will the wine develop? What was the general opinion of the finished product? Were the fermentations normal? What were the sugar contents like? These and many other questions are being discussed and asked by everyone dealing with the vintage at this time. We shall cover this subject more fully in a later chapter, but first we must look ahead at all the hard work and toil to be completed before September of the following year.

If an artist were to paint the vineyards of the Douro valley at the end of October, when the leaves have changed to the most vivid of red, yellow and purple hues, many who do not know the district at this time of year would never believe the colours were real. For the student of viticulture, it is the time to learn the different types of vines with their many varied leaves, as it is possible to pick them out in a vineyard simply by their colours, particularly the well-known varieties such as the Tintas, Tourigas and Malvasias.

The soil is dry and arid after many weeks of hot scorching sun, and the vines by now have lost some of their leaves, so the first work to be done in November is the *escava d'agua*: the digging of trenches around the vines in order to catch as much rain as possible to water the roots during the coming winter months.

Pruning

During this period, a group of very specially skilled workers arrive at the *quintas* to prune the vines. These workers are known as *podadores* (pruners)—they are regarded as a special breed owing to their excellent capacity for imbibing the local table wine. It is a known fact that a good pruner will drink a minimum of five litres of wine per day and, should the pruning continue into the month of December when the temperature begins to fall, *bagaceira* (the local *marc*) will also be included in the day's menu.

The art of pruning is passed down from father to son, and normally the same party or family will come every year to the same *quinta*. This is one of the most important skills, as a bad pruner can ruin the vine and its future production. The system of pruning in the Douro vineyards would appear to be very similar to the Médoc system and is probably the most ruthless form of pruning practised anywhere, as the vine is pruned right back with cutter and saw, leaving never more than one long *barra* or bearer on each side.

These are always chosen from the main and lowest boughs, as it is essential to keep the trunk or *cavalo* as short as possible. The two *barras* are then tied to the lower wire strung along the rows, the left being the *mãe* or mother and the right one the *filha* or daughter. Each bearer normally has only two or three eyes, as the Douro vine lives in an area where moisture is at a premium and its main effort in life must be expended in producing a few high-quality bunches of grapes, which is all that the climate, certainly in the upper part of the valley, will support.

Those vines which grow on trellises with long stems and widely flung tendrils are not legally used for port wine, as much of the strength and quality has been expended before the sap finally reaches the actual fruit and leaves. In the Minho and Vinho Verde districts, the vines grow on trellises and up the trees to a great height, but the resultant wine is acid, light and low in alcoholic strength: excellent of its kind, but as different from port as a wine could be.

Generally, in the early part of March, the vines begin to bleed. This is caused by the absorption of water by the vine after the cold winter period has ended and the soil and air temperatures have begun to rise again. It can also be caused by the expansion of gas bubbles of air and carbon dioxide in the sap of the roots, and coincides with the period when the new young roots are formed annually by the vine. This bleeding is rapid and of short duration.

Terracing and replanting

February and March are busy months, as this is the time when the soil is prepared for the planting of the American vine, the grafting (a year later), and the preparation of new vineyards. From the description of the soil, it becomes evident that the preparation of the vineyards is a tremendous labour as well as a costly one, owing to the steepness of the mountains and the hardness of the soil itself. Terrace-building forms the major task, for these hold the soil in position during the rainy season; up to a short while ago, these were entirely 'dry', built by hand, using the actual schistous rock with no cement or binding.

It has never been an easy method of cultivation and it is still not easy, for one seldom comes across slopes of less than 20° gradient and, more frequently, in the Cima Corgo, vines are found on gradients varying between 40° and 70°. In fact, 90 per cent of the demarcated area has gradients of over 30°, which are reckoned to be the maximum workable limit for construction of terraces and vine cultivation in other wine-growing countries. So it has been under rather adverse conditions that this, the oldest, demarcated area has survived and flourished to represent a major factor in the Portuguese economy: an economy which has to be safeguarded in rapidly changing conditions, where labour is no longer cheap nor easily available and machinery has still to be developed to solve the basic problems of the terrain.

In this extremely mountainous area, two types of terracing have been constructed for the vines: horizontal and inclined terracing. The latter is usually wider and therefore cheaper to construct. In both cases it would be impossible, economically, to mechanise cultivation without first re-converting the vineyards, as the terraces themselves are separated by the dry rock walls and joined by steps to facilitate the movement of the workers. To keep production costs down and counteract the labour shortage, certain forms of mechanisation will be necessary in the future, even in this difficult terrain.

The advantage of horizontal terracing in the Douro is twofold: firstly, that it has a better capacity for water retention in the drought zones, and secondly that it will be easier to make use of the Emjambeur tractor in the future, once the terraces are re-built and widened and the space between the vines is increased. This machine, a tractor on stilts which straddles the vines, has proved very successful. It will be used for spraying the vines, digging between the rows, and other viticultural purposes. Where the land is neither as rocky nor as steep, as in the Lower Corgo, the possibility of converting the vineyards to the West German and Swiss system of planting the vines in rows and following the line of the gradient is being studied. The Douro policy is one of adaptation and improvement, rather than radical change, for it is felt that it would be a great error to do anything that could possibly alter the basic character and quality of a product which must maintain the high standards necessary and, indeed, improve on them when possible.

Thus today, the monster 120- to 180-horsepower bulldozer has appeared in the Douro vineyards, equipped with blades, ripper and rake. Before starting on the modern method of terracing, it must be decided what width the slopes will allow the final platform to be, i.e. 3, 4, 5, or 6 metres. The last width can only be constructed when the slope does not exceed a 30° gradient. For gradients of more than 40°, a platform of 4 metres width is normally found to be the most suitable, to include the maximum number of vines, as well as sufficient space for vehicles to manoeuvre. In fact, terraces of this width can be made on very rocky soil and gradients up to 65° and, provided that the annual rainfall does not exceed 800 mm, there is no need to add a support wall, as the soil and rock which have been moved will soon grow natural vegetation to bind the terrace together. Since 1967, when this system was first tested, there has not been one single incident of land-fall, and the natural vegetation, having a short season of flowering, does not detract from the nourishment that the soil can give the vines.

To summarise, on gradients from 40° to 65° with terraces of 4 metres in width, normally two rows of vines are planted. Those between 30° and 40° with terraces up to 5 metres have three rows of vines; and those of gradients between 20° and 30°, four rows on platforms of between 5·5 and 6·5 metres in width. Only two rows, and these rather narrow, can be planted on the 3 metre wide terraces.

During the construction of the terracing, it is important that access roads between 4 and 5 metres wide and of a gradient not exceeding 15° should be included obliquely on the slope which, again, should link up the terraces. Each terrace must retain the same width for its entire length, although there can be complete terraces of different widths on the same slope. All this essential construction is a costly business and the final figure does not include the small loss of land which is caused by sloping the modern terrace walls, against the old vertical dry walls built in the past.

Having temporarily set aside the vineyard labourer, with his hoe, dynamite and hammer, we continue with the bulldozer and the preparation of the soil. This machine breaks up the soil with the attached blade and ripper, but even then it is occasionally beaten by the huge schistous rocks, and only dynamite can be effective. When all the larger rocks have been cleared and removed, a rake replaces the blade to flatten the surface.

Fertilisers are applied during the 'ploughing', the actual type depending on the nature of the soil. In the old days, these fertilisers were exclusively of the humus nature, but this has become impractical due to the lack of labour available in the area. Today they are largely made up of organic matter such as fish meal, and inorganic fertilisers. These can be divided into three main headings of phosphorus and nitrogenous substances and potassium. The first includes phosphates, super phosphates and phosphate of ammonia; the second, sulphate of ammonia, phosphate of ammonia, sodium, calcium or potassium nitrates; and the third potassium nitrate, potassium sulphate and potassium chloride. All these fertilisers must be used with care and understanding; otherwise the farmer will find his yield much increased with an inevitable fall in the quality of the grape. It is a general rule that nitrate is only applied 15 to 30 days after the 'ploughing'.

Once the land is prepared, the one-year-old American stock is then planted in manually prepared holes 1·4 metres deep, and due regard to the spacing between the rows and vines is necessary to allow for the future possibility of mechanical aids. Formerly the vines were planted 1 metre apart and with 1 metre between the rows, but today the basic formula, varying according to the width of the terrace, is:

1·3 metres between rows × 1·4 metres between vines
1·4 metres between rows × 1·3 metres between vines
1·5 metres between rows × 1·3 metres between vines

but in some cases some farmers will plant with greater widths between the vines and rows, depending upon the geographical position of their *quinta*.

The new vineyards presuppose the use of the Emjambeur tractor, which can operate between rows of from 0·90 metres to 1·50 metres apart. Although studies continue with a view to adapting present machinery to the difficult local conditions, there is no doubt that it will always be hard to achieve the excellent results obtained when this machinery is used on flatter and more receptive ground.

Grafting

The American vine is then allowed to establish itself for one further year and, in the early part of the second year of its life, it is cut back to the root stalk and the national vine is grafted on to it. It is sometimes hard to believe that having planted one thousand of these vines in the Upper Douro, they will possibly only ever produce one pipe of port a year, or, shall we say, a mere seven hundred bottles!

The grafting is carried out by yet another 'family' from a different district. The cuttings from the national vines are taken from specially selected ones which have been chosen to continue the style of port made at the *quinta*, and these vines are left unpruned so that they can be used only for grafting. This is another craft of vital importance in the vineyards, as success or failure of future production is largely dependent on the expertise of the *enxertador*.

The soil is removed from around the base of the American vine, which is cut off one *palmo*, 20 centimetres, below the top of the soil (the *palmo*, or palm of the hand, is still in general use here as a unit of measurement). It is next split with a knife and the national vine inserted, bound tightly with raffia and then covered again with the soil. A small stick is then placed above the earth to show that the *enxerto* or grafting has been successfully completed.

It is maintained by A. I. Bertold, Professor of Viticulture and Oenology at the University of Stellenbosch, that through grafting on to the American stock, the European vines have become increasingly susceptible to disease and pests, and that grafting, therefore, is the cause of the severe fight which the European wine farmers must put up today to fend off the enemies of the vine.

Growth and spraying

From the beginning of April, in normal years, the eyes on the stem begin to swell and the green buds burst and develop rapidly. According to the old theory, it takes from twenty to thirty days from the time the vines begin to bleed until the buds start to open. These rapidly grow into young shoots and by the begining of May, when the first spraying, with Bordeaux mixture, takes place, and each individual shoot is dusted with sulphur, the flowering process follows and the embryo bunches of grapes appear in miniature, breaking into flower.

The visitor will go into rhapsodies over this natural development, but the farmer crosses his fingers and prays, as the weather at this period is vital. Cold and heavy rains can affect the process of germination of the pollen grains, and cause the flowers to drop before they have been properly fertilised, resulting in scraggy bunches with very few grapes. Strong winds can also have the same effect, and it is not uncommon after such conditions to find many bunches virtually in embryo with tiny dried-up grapes.

After the flowering, the spraying of the vines continues at varying intervals during the next two or three months, the actual number of sprayings depending entirely upon the weather during the growing period. As this operation is essentially to protect the vines from attacks of mildew, it might need to be continued until the beginning of August, but in normal hot summers, this is seldom necessary and no spraying takes place within a month of the start of the vintage.

Around the 24th June, St John's Day, one begins to see the first tracing of colour on the grape skins. This is charmingly referred to as the arrival of the *pintor*, or 'painter', in the vineyards. The exact time cannot be general throughout the valley, because of the microclimates and position of the *quintas*, but from that moment on, the grapes begin to swell and ripen until the time of picking, which usually starts about the third week in September.

There are occasions when the growth of the leaf has been too prolific, so in August a proportion of these are removed to allow the ripening of the bunches. However, care has to be taken not to remove too many of the leaves, as they contain the original sugar, which then passes through to the berry and is a vital component of any grape.

The vineyards are kept weed-free by occasionally turning the soil over between the vines. To date, this is still done by man or mule; obviously, it will be a great financial and labour-saving operation when the mechanical plough is used. There is seldom a day in the whole year when some form of cultivation and maintenance is not being carried out in the vineyards, despite the varying climatic conditions of extreme heat and cold. But this is all necessary to obtain the top quality every farmer strives for in the end. His satisfaction comes with the vintage in September, when he sees the beautiful, pungent and colourful must fermenting in his installations, and knows he has done all he can to achieve the best results.

Implements

The climax of the year, the vintage, will be dealt with in more detail in the following chapter but, before concluding this one, we must first look at the tools used in the Douro, which are few and simple.

Virtually the only tool used throughout the year is the *enchada de bicos compridos*, a double-pronged fork-cum-hoe. The normal length of the handle of the implement is 4·5 *palmos* (90 cm). It is used for digging around the vines, especially in the

late autumn in preparation for the heavy rains as well as for weeding and other tasks. Its smaller brother, the *enchada de bicos curtos*, with a *5-palmo* (100 cm) handle but shorter teeth, is generally used for vegetable plots kept by farmers.

The *sacho de bico* or single-bladed narrow hoe has three uses in the vineyards. In February, it is used for marking the 'line' for planting the American stocks in a new plantation. Later in

November and December, it is used for clearing the area around the vines before pruning, and, having a 7-*palmo* handle, it is also used to steady the large basket which is carried on the neck of the worker during the vintage. This basket, the *cesto vindimo*, holds about 60 kg of grapes.

The *sachola* or *enchada de raza*, with a 4·5-*palmo* handle, is a useful implement for weeding and for general clearing of the vineyards and the surrounding ground near the farmer's buildings. Finally, there is the *martelo* or hammer. This may seem a

strange tool to be used in the vineyard until one realises the type of soil in the Douro, but then it becomes logical as a farming tool. It is used to break up the schistous rock before planting the

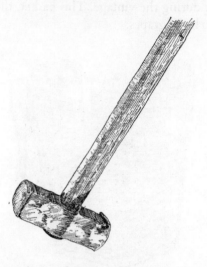

American vine. It has a short handle—3·5 *palmos*—and is very heavy-headed. With this small collection of implements, crude but highly efficient and suitable for the work, the vineyards of the Douro have been maintained for over three centuries.

5

The Vintage

Preparation and care in production

The vintage: *a vindima, la vendemmia, la vindimia, la récolte, die Weinlese*, no matter in what language, or in which country, is still the culmination of one year's toil and anxiety for the farmer and the completion of the annual cycle of the vine. There is always that personal feeling over the final outcome of the crop, and one can never get away from the one factor that rules the grapes and the vineyards—the weather. Although this may be the Englishman's topic of conversation, to the Douro farmer it is even more important: a sudden hailstorm in July or August in the Douro valley can, in ten minutes, rip through a vineyard and destroy a twenty-pipe crop. Again, too much sun without a cooling shower can burn the grapes and reduce the yield; too much rain will create eventual problems coupled with diseases, mildew and subsequent reduction of the natural sugar content of the grape; while excess cold will retard the maturation. These challenges, however, keep the producers on their toes, instilling into them a need for care in the preparation and production at the vintage. As the saying goes, 'God gives us the grape, let us do our utmost to produce a good wine.'

The date of starting the vintage in the Douro is of vital importance, and, as always, depends upon the weather. It can vary according to the geographical situation of the vineyard itself, owing to the aforementioned microclimates, and, while in the Upper Corgo the vintage might begin, say, on 20th September, it could start two or three weeks later in some parts of the Lower

Corgo. In 1972 it only started in October, and finished in late November, the latest date since 1892. However, a great deal of hard work must be accomplished within the few weeks prior to this date by the shipper, as vineyards must be visited and crops and installations examined. The final date of picking must also be decided upon, depending entirely upon the percentage of natural sugar in the grape at that time.

Formerly, all farmers made their wine in their own vineyards and the shipper purchased these wines from him, having already supplied the *aguardente* and an employee of his company, to oversee and control the whole operation. Today, as the majority of shippers have their own production centres, the age-old treading is fast disappearing, the grapes being purchased from the farmers and transported by lorry to the shipper's installations, usually situated in their own *quintas*. There are still some farmers who own large properties, and who have installed their own mechanical presses and fermenting vats, and these farmers will then make their own wine and sell the finished product to the shipper.

Maximum cleanliness is essential in all the various utensils used throughout the vintage, which include vats, casks, pumps, hoses, cans, presses and any other object which will come into contact with either the must or the finished wine. All are thoroughly disinfected with sulphur crystals, but possibly the most important one to remember is the container itself in which the wine will be kept in the *adegas*, after the vintage, for some months before being transported down to Vila Nova de Gaia, and the shipper's lodges in the following spring.

These containers can be upstanding vats (*balseiros*); tonnels (*tuneis*) made from oak, chestnut, or Brazilian mahogany; cement vats (*cubas de cimento*); or casks. All the large containers have a small door or inlet (*portinhola*), to allow a man to enter and clean them when necessary. On inspection day these *portinholas* are removed, and the shipper, or whoever is inspecting the containers for him, sticks his head in and gently inhales while beating the outside of the container to rouse the fumes. Inhaling 'gently' is the operative word because a sharp and deep inhalation of this tremendous concentration of fumes could well overcome one! The stronger and cleaner the fumes, the better the condition of the container, as it will mean that it has been completely airtight since the time the wine was removed.

There are two methods normally used to keep these containers in perfect condition. The first is to leave a small quantity of port at the bottom left over from the previous vintage, and the second is to dry it out completely, leaving a stick of sulphur there. The *portinhola* should be completely closed and sealed to maintain the required freshness during the container's period of rest. This is the responsibility of the farmer, and, although a bad or unclean vat is seldom found, we have discovered on one or two occasions that a *portinhola* has been left out, and the said vat was being used as a chicken run. The feathered friends were in excellent health, sober and well-nurtured, but unfortunately, the vat was condemned.

A bad container can be mildewed, dirty, sour or vinegary and, should it leak, the smell of goat fat can sometimes be detected, as this is often used to fill in the cracked staves. It would taint the wine immediately, so prevention, obviously, is better than cure. A simple method of cleaning a dirty or sour vat is to wash it out with a 20 per cent solution of carbonate of sodium or potassium and to repeat this until it is clean and sound. Should the container be very bad, the following treatment is the most effective. First wash it out with a 10 per cent sodium carbonate solution in hot water, then wash well with cold water. After this, apply a 10 per cent sulphuric acid solution, not forgetting to add the sulphuric acid after the water has been run into the container, or the workman could be burned by the splashing effect created by pouring water onto the acid. Finally, 1 kilo of lime, or some similar alkali, in 5 litres of water, should then be used to wash out the vat, and, when it is completely dry, a stick of sulphur placed at the bottom and the *portinhola* firmly closed. When a really bad, vinegary cask is found, there is only one thing to do with it and that is to burn it—or use it for storing vinegar.

To prevent a brand-new wooden container giving wine a

'woody' taste, it must be washed out first with a solution of 500 grammes of salt to 10 litres of water. A more drastic method is to treat it with 3 to 5 kilos of lime in 550 litres of water, which will create a very high temperature and burn the surface of the new wood. Afterwards it will, obviously, have to be washed well with water. A third method, seldom used, but an historic and superstitious one, is that of mixing 2 or 3 kilos of ground oak bark with 10 litres of water and adding to this 2 kilos of sodium carbonate, leaving it until the bark is completely dissolved, and then using the solution.

Today, the use of cement containers in various forms is becoming more necessary as the high cost and scarcity of good wood leaves the shipper no alternative. Some are lined with glass tiles, but generally speaking these have proved to be somewhat unsuccessful over a period of time, as the glass joins can deteriorate and create pockets of breeding grounds for bacteria. They are now mostly painted with a special neutral plastic paint which has proved very successful, as it is very simple to wash the container with water, thoroughly dry, and then use it again either for white or red wine immediately afterwards. When the cement containers are not painted, a 10 per cent tartaric acid solution in water is normally applied to the inside walls to protect the wine attacking the cement surface and preventing a possible fungoid growth. A second method would be to apply a 25 per cent potassium silicate solution in water to prevent the wine coming in direct contact with the cement, and should this not be effective, a second, stronger solution at 50 per cent could be applied.

Often it is necessary to use a container for white wine when it has previously been used for red, and the most effective method of removing colour from the inside walls is to wash them with 2 kg of sodium carbonate dissolved in 10 litres of boiling water. A stronger treatment is the use of 0·5 litres of hydrochloric acid to 10 litres of water. The container must be washed out immediately with fresh water and then with a solution of 100 grammes of permanganate of potassium to 10 litres of water, followed by a second wash of fresh water, until it becomes completely colourless.

We do not apologise to our readers for this rather tedious portion of the chapter, as hygiene and cleanliness right from the start is all-important.

Picking

Having dealt in detail with the preparation and care of pre-vintage work, we now follow on with the picking, pressing and fermentation. It is an old tradition in the Douro that the same *roga*, or group of harvesters, returns to the same *quinta* year after year; possibly even with three generations in one family working at the same time. Tradition, coupled with parental respect, is very strong in the Douro. This can be illustrated by an incident which occurred when an American journalist was looking for a family of wine growers of four generations, to photograph and write an article on that family. When the elder three members were asked to sit, and the great-grandson to stand, in the front of the group, the reply was, 'Only the head of the family sits, sir, and we, the younger generation, stand.' There was no servility in the remark—purely respect.

It is a gay reunion of the shippers and farmers and *rogas*; a family atmosphere prevails and many old tales of previous vintages are passed on from generation to generation. Some amusing, some sad or even romantic, they all contain a form of education, not read in books. So many 'old wives' tales' are scorned today, but little do the ones who scorn them realise what truth and experience lie behind them. They were not invented, they were evolved. Here is an example. The shipper must wait for 'two winters and a summer' before he is in a position to declare a vintage port, as so much can happen to the young wine during that period, no matter how magnificent it may be at the time of production.

The pickers are a hard-working band: their daily hours start at sunrise and finish at sunset, because no grape waits for anyone once it is mature and ready to be picked. The women cut the bunches of grapes with short knives or secateurs and sort them, while the younger generation transfer the laden small baskets to the large ones, the *cesto vindimo,* which are placed at strategic points to be carried away, when full, by the men.

Whenever geographically possible, these baskets are taken to the presses by tractor or lorry, but often this is impossible owing to the narrow terraces and the steepness of the mountainside. The men in long lines carry these laden baskets, weighing up to 65 kilos, on the nape of their necks. A sack is fitted on the man's head, covering his back. A log, covered in sacking, is then placed on the nape of his neck and held in position by a cloth strap around his forehead. The basket is then placed on this log, the weight being distributed between the forehead, the nape of the neck and the shoulders. The same principle is used all over the world in various forms; it is the way American Indian squaws carry their children, for instance. The balance is normally so well adjusted that it is hardly necessary to hold the basket at all. The long, dusty march to the presses is led by a foreman blowing a whistle to keep time, and sometimes the men accompany him by playing flutes and triangles, beating drums and singing. The work is hard, but the vintage time is usually considered a gay part of the year and there is much laughter and singing!

The *rogador* or overseer is responsible for the general welfare and discipline of the workers; normally he returns to the same *quinta* every year. At Croft's, the same man has been in charge for over fifty years, and has become part of the 'family'.

The grapes arriving at the reception tanks are weighed and the *lagrima* (tear)—the Douro term for the natural sugar of the grape—is taken and registered by a modern refractometer. This machine automatically 'weighs' the sugar in the juice and gives the most accurate reading of all modern appliances. The red and white grapes are, naturally, kept apart, as are the larger *quintas* and regions with their great varieties of grapes giving each individual *quinta* its special style of wine. The grapes are then emptied into the silos and screw-fed into the pressing machine.

Formerly, in the Lower Corgo district, the official weight of grapes laid down by the Casa do Douro to produce one pipe of port was 750 kilos, while in the Upper Corgo, 950 kilos was the official figure, owing to the lower yield and finer quality. Today 750 kilos of grapes per pipe of port is the official figure throughout the whole of the Douro district, which does not favour the shipper who buys mostly in the Upper Corgo, as the price paid to the farmer is set in terms of kilos and not pipes. However, this is the law, and all contracts between farmer and shipper are based on this quantity.

Treading

Before we pass on to the modern methods of vinification, let us linger for a few moments on the old-fashioned and fast disappearing treading with the bare foot. The *lagar* or treading tank in which this operation takes place is generally constructed from solid granite in varying sizes, in which anything up to twenty or thirty pipes of wine can be made. They are normally square in shape, the walls being roughly 75 cm in height and occasionally beautifully carved by hand. Others are made with slate walls, but these can never compare with the splendour of the granite ones.

When the *lagars* are filled with grapes, the men line up, in their shorts, on the opposite walls, arm in arm facing each other. The *rogador* has meticulously inspected their legs and feet, which have been scrubbed to shining point with soap and water. The stage is now set for the ceremony of the *corte* or cutting of the fresh grapes, and, at a given signal, they step into the mass, forcing their legs to the bottom. The official number of treaders per pipe of grapes in the *lagar* should be two, but forty men in a twenty-pipe *lagar* would give little space for movement and freedom, so there are generally about half that. They start marching in unison, crushing the bunches and treading as methodically as soldiers, with the foreman standing outside shouting *esquerda–direita* (left–right) like an army sergeant. To break the monotony he sometimes changes his command to *um–dois* (one–two)! When the two lines meet, they then swivel round to cut the *lagar* in the opposite direction. It sounds so simple to tread grapes, but having personally tried it, we must admit that it is really hard going with the depth of the mountain of grapes being well above the knees. The stain from the colour of the red grape skins can last for two or three days on one's legs.

The *corte* continues for at least two hours, or until the grapes are properly crushed and the juice floats evenly on top of the mass. At that moment the signal for *liberdade* (freedom) is given, which is received with a mighty cheer from the treaders who break away from the military discipline and dance (always treading) around the *lagar*, up to their thighs in purple grape juice, singing and shouting, accompanied by the band of concertinas, triangles and the ever-present drum. The hard work and merriment continues day and night, the spirits of the treaders being kept up by frequent tots of *bagaceira* (the local *marc* or *grappa*), and cigarettes given by the owners of the *quinta*. The women dance outside the *lagar*, with any of the male fraternity who are not occupied with the actual treading or together, as there are few men available. It is interesting that in the past there were some districts in the Douro where the men refused to tread unless their womenfolk accompanied them in the *lagar*, but today this is seldom seen.

The must begins to ferment, becoming darker and more purple (in red wines) as the natural colour is extracted from the skins; and the treading continues until the must is fermenting strongly. Boards are then placed across the *lagar* to allow men to stand on them with *macacos*, or wooden paddles, and keep the fermentation alive and fresh by turning the must over and working continuously from above. During this period the sugar content of the grape is being converted into alcohol, and the sweetness is constantly measured. When the desired sweetness is reached the must is drawn off into the awaiting vats and containers where *aguardente* (grape alcohol at 77 per cent by volume) is immediately added to arrest the fermentation—and port is born.

Modern vinification

After this short description of the old-fashioned and age-old method of vinification, we shall return to this mechanical age of crushing by machine, and modern methods. Up to around 1960, virtually the entire production of port was crushed by the human foot. Many magnificent ports have been made over the years by this method: the 1847s, 1896s, 1912s, 1927s, 1945s and other famous vintages. We now wonder if these wines could have been improved. Professor Amerine, the great American oenologist, in an address to the Institute of the Masters of Wine in July 1969, stated that the human foot, contrary to what we have been taught, was perhaps the worst crusher of grapes, as opposed to the best! It was not shaped to crush grapes but to walk on and, in his belief, if the Good Lord had wished us to have feet solely to crush grapes with, He would surely have designed something better!

The fact remains, however, that as far as one knows, wines have been trodden in stone, wooden and other containers since the beginning of time and it was not until the early 1950s that a real study of the problems produced pressing machinery that was a great deal better than anything that has been available before. In Portugal there was little interest in using the older machines, as labour was cheap and plentiful in the vineyards and very few of the small vineyards had electricity. Mains electricity has become generally available only quite recently.

During the early 1960s labour began to be a problem. A gradual trickle of emigrants from all over Portugal started to leave for France and Germany, where wages were considerably higher; this trickle became an ever-increasing stream and labour became more and more difficult to obtain. The shortage was further aggravated by conscription; many of the young men having to do their military service in the overseas provinces of Portugal, where the length of service was indeterminate. The resultant shortage of labour forced many of the port shippers to study mechanisation in order to produce their wine at all.

The machines considered most suitable for port wine production were of French design, and today they are produced under licence by two manufacturers in Torres Vedras, north of Lisbon. To explain the modern method of pressing the grapes we must start with the electrically driven screw feeder, operating at the base of a V-shaped reception tank, which carries the bunches of grapes in a steady flow into the crushing and stemming machine, an upright cylinder about 1 metre in diameter. An axle runs down the centre of this, on to which are fixed, at regular intervals, four iron trays, each one containing a series of angled blades. The axle is also driven by an electric motor from above, revolving at an extremely high speed. The bunches fall on to these revolving trays, the angled blades smashing them, and the centrifugal force hurling the resultant mush against the

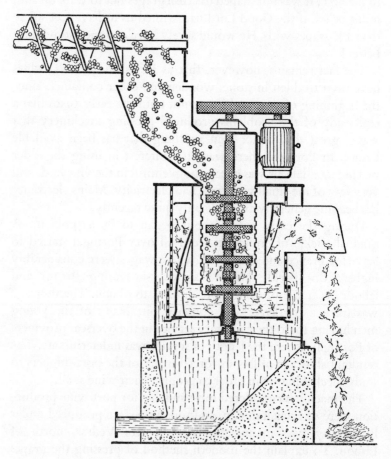

corrugated internal walls of the cylinder, avoiding, however, breaking the pips, which would give the must a bitter taste owing to the release of essential oils which, once there, can never be got rid of. These internal walls are vertically movable, and can be adjusted to open or close by simply turning a small wheel on the outside of the crusher.

As the stalks contain much of the tannin, it is necessary to keep all these in the crusher in a dry, hot year, when they are

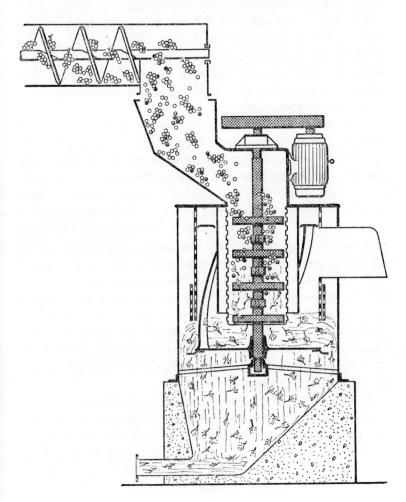

brown and dry, so as to extract the maximum of tannin to produce a balanced wine. However, in a 'green year', when there has been little sun and the tannin content in the stems could possibly be too high, a certain proportion of these must be discarded, sometimes up to two-thirds of the total. Here the adjustable walls play their part; the portion of discarded stems can be regulated by opening or closing the aperture, and the angled blades cause a sufficient draught to blow the discarded stems upwards and outwards through a hatch.

The must continues to fall from tray to tray, until, in a pulverised form, it reaches the bottom of the machine. When crushing the red grapes, even at this early stage, the colour from the skins already begins to appear. The must is then pumped via plastic tubes, straight to the fermenting tanks situated in the cool *adegas*.

As far as can be ascertained, the fermenting tanks of the kind now used in the Douro were first used in Algeria, where the system is known as the Ducellier system, and possibly earlier in the wine-producing State of California. These tanks are usually constructed in cement and painted internally with an inert paint, already described, which greatly facilitates the maintenance and hygiene, as well as the change-over from red to white grapes. This simply constructed container usually holds between 25 and 30 pipes of must. It has an open trough at the top and within this, at one corner, there is another small one for the use of a water escape valve. The only two operative parts used in this simple operation are the water valve and the autovinificator. This is merely a cylinder, 1·2 m in length and 0·6 m in width, including an outer sleeve. Inside the enclosed fermenting tank, there is a fixed open fibro-cement tube, the top of which appears in the large open trough.

The must is pumped into the tank direct from the crushing machine, through a 0·6 m aperture, and filled to within some 40 cm from the top. The autovinificator is then inserted into the hole and clamped down with four wing nuts, and the water escape valve is filled with the required amount of water (the quantity of water is regulated by the amount of must to be

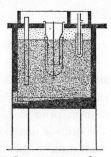 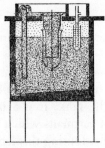

Diagram of cross-section of fermenting tank. Must is pumped from the crusher into the tank and filled to approximately 45 cm between level of must and roof of tank. Autovinificator is screwed into large hole and fixed with wing nuts.

Must starts to ferment. Carbon dioxide gases produced in empty confined space build up to such a pressure as to force the must down. Must can only escape through tube and spill into top of tank.

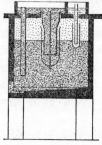 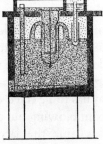

When the gas pressure reaches the right level it forces the water out through the top of the valve allowing gases to escape.

Pressure is released. Must automatically pours back into autovinificator at great speed and is sprinkled over the 'Blanket' or 'Manta' formed by the continuous fermentation.

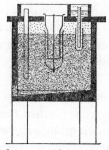 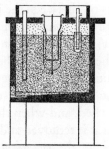

The whole process then starts up again. Natural sugar from the grapes is automatically turning into alcohol thus reducing the sweetness. When it reaches the required level the must is drawn off and AD or grape brandy is added.

The sooner the fermentation is arrested the sweeter the wine, the later the fermentation is arrested, the drier the wine.

fermented in the tank) and inserted in another hole in the small trough.

Generally speaking, in normal temperature conditions, at around 16°C, the must begins to ferment fairly soon after it enters the tank. It is a natural fermentation produced by the yeasts or ferments which are found on the outside of the skin of the grape. During this fermentation, which usually lasts for two or three days, carbon dioxide gas is produced and accumulates in the space between the must and the top of the inside of the tank, and the pressure from this expanding gas forces the must downwards. The only possible escape for it is now the open tube in the tank, and so the must begins to appear at the top end, and starts to fill the large trough. If this operation were allowed to continue, the gases would eventually force all the must out of the tank, and all would be lost. This is when the water escape valve comes into operation: when the gas pressure reaches a certain level it forces the water out through the top of the valve, allowing the gases to escape into the air. The pressure is so great that a lid has to be fixed on top of the valve so as to prevent the water from blowing out over the *adega*.

By this time the large open trough is nearly filled with fermenting must, and the small trough with water from the escape valve. The gases having escaped, and with no pressure in the tank, both the must and the water flow back, the first through the autovinificator into the tank and the second back into the escape valve. As the must flows back through the autovinificator, it sprays out between the inner and outer sleeves of the cylinder, thus airing it, keeping the fermentation fresh, and the *manta* or 'blanket' which forms on the surface continually on the move. Once the tank is filled the whole procedure starts up again and repeats itself.

In the meantime the sugar content is being carefully tested and checked, and when the required degree is reached the auto-vinificator is removed and the must is drawn off into the waiting vats, where the *aguardente* is immediately added to arrest this fermentation. This suspends the action of the micro-organisms, which cannot work at above a certain, slightly variable, alcoholic level, usually about 16 per cent. Any sugar remaining is left in the wine. For instance if the original grape sugar is 14 per cent and the fermenting must is drawn off when it has reached 6 per cent, 8 per cent will be left in sugar. An easy formula to remember is: 'The earlier the fermentation is arrested, the sweeter the port'.

There is a means of controlling the temperature of the fermentation in the tanks by pumping cold water through pipes inserted down the syphon tube, but unless this water is prechilled, coming from the Douro river in the summer months, it will, in the end, have little effect. In our experience at Croft's over a period of more than ten years with these fermentation tanks, the temperatures have never risen above 28°C. When the fermentation is too rapid, in very hot years, the necessary 'work' to extract all the colour from the skins (in the case of red grapes) is considerably reduced, and if the temperature begins to approach danger level at 32°C, tartaric acid should be immediately added to control it, as the conditions produced over that temperature, are ideal for the growth of various bacteria, especially the *mannite*.

The fermentation of white port is never allowed to continue too long in contact with the skins which, when golden brown at vintage time, could produce too much colour, and this obviously would spoil the appearance of white port. In order to guarantee a really light white port, the *bica aberta* method is occasionally used. Strictly speaking, this method is only used for making white table wines, as the fermenting juice hardly comes in contact with the skins at all, and the juice is then transferred to another container to continue its natural fermentation. This method is accepted only for white ports, but it is necessary if you want a very light-coloured white port, which is desirable in itself and also as a blending wine for cheap tawny ports, where the lighter the white port, the less is needed. The grapes for white port can acquire quite a lot of colour and any substantial contact with the skin produces a wine that is gold-coloured.

One of the main advantages of the enclosed fermenting tank is that the whole process of fermentation is conducted in a virtually airtight container where hardly any oxygen exists, thus averting many of the dangers of aerobic bacteria developing, as they cannot survive in a carbon dioxide atmosphere.

Although the type of fermenting tank which we have described is the one normally seen in the Douro and used, for instance, at Croft's Quinta da Roeda, there are other methods. Sandeman have a magnificent complex of stainless steel tanks, while Cockburn use, as well as the 'open-tank' method, the Movimosto process. The open tank, or *remontage*, is not generally used as it requires considerably more labour. The system is very simple: the grapes, when crushed, are pumped into open cement vats varying in size, but normally holding between ten and fifteen thousand litres of must. As soon as fermentation begins, the solids are automatically pushed to the surface; a pump is then connected to the bottom of the tank and the liquid must is pumped up by tube and sprayed over the *manta* or 'blanket'. This pump must be strong as it has to spray the *manta* with enough power to break it up and to immerse it in the must on which it floats.

This keeps the *manta* fresh and continues the action of the fermentation of the solids, an important point in the extraction of the colour. This system has the one advantage of being closely associated with the old treading principle in the *lagars* which allows a very complete oxidation of the musts. It is also fairly effective from the point of view of temperature control, by the fact that the *manta*, which is much hotter than the must, is continually being sprayed with cooler liquid, which, to a certain extent, slows down the fermentation and gives more work to the wine. The problem, however, is that of colour, as, unless there is virtually continuous *remontage*, the colour of the wines tends to suffer in comparison with those produced by the Ducellier system.

The Movimosto system is a simple solution produced by Cockburn Smithes in 1966 to meet the needs of the small farmer, who at that time was suffering from the lack of local labour brought about by emigration to France and Germany. The machine was extremely well thought-out, and simply applied the *remontage* system to the stone treading tank. Electrically operated by a small two-horse-power motor, the inlet pipe was placed in a corner of the *lagar* behind a protective mesh screen to keep the solids away and allowing only the liquid must to penetrate the mesh. From time to time the must was then sprayed on top of the *manta* to obtain the same result as the open-tank method. However, both these aforementioned systems had the defect that if the motor and pressure of the spraying was too weak, the *manta* and solids were not sufficiently broken up to produce the perfect fermentation.

To conclude these paragraphs on the vintage and fermentation, we should add some figures. The specific gravity of the must, before fermentation, is normally between 1·091 (12·3 per cent alcohol or 11·91° Baumé) and 1·100 (13·9 per cent alcohol or 13·11° Baumé) in the case of red port musts, and 1·091 (12·3 per cent alcohol or 11·91° Baumé) and 1·095 (13·1 per cent alcohol or 12·5° Baumé) for white port musts. In a year of average quality, the total acidity, given as tartaric acid per litre, would be between 3·9 and 6 grammes, and the tannin between 400 and 600 mg per litre. There is remarkably little difference in the analysis of red and white musts in these respects. The fermentation is allowed to continue until the specific gravity reaches 1·045 (6·2° Baumé). If the must is analysed immediately before being drawn off, there is little change in the results, apart from the fall in specific gravity, and in the case of red ports, a sharp increase in colour. Usually, but not invariably, an increase in the tannin content of about 60 mg per litre is noted, but little change in the pH or total acid content. The volatile acidity rarely rises above 0·035 grammes acetic acid per 100 ml.

It is unusual to add anything to the must at this stage, apart from a small quantity of metabisulphate during the crushing for reasons of disinfection and control of the fermentation. At one time, citric acid was considered to be advantageous, but it seems to have achieved little or nothing. However, tartaric acid is sometimes added as a corrective of the fixed acid should this be low, in order to reduce the possibility of any bacterial development.

When finally the grapes are pressed and fermented and the wine fortified and lying in its containers, the *roga* gather to say farewell until the following year. A girl is selected to present the owner's wife with the traditional *rama*, a beautifully decorated cane with vine leaves, coloured paper streamers and the inevitable bunch of grapes. This is hand-made by the pickers and workers themselves. It is blessed by the local priest, and will remain in the *quinta* until the following vintage when the same 'family' hope to reappear. Food and wine is offered all round, and after much cheering and friendly chat they leave, singing and dancing, and return to their village, possibly a few kilometres away. A happy time, a period full of memories, coupled with hard work and hopes for the future.

Brandy (aguardente)

This product ought not really to be called brandy, as we find that it causes confusion in the general public's mind; they immediately think of France and cognac. It is in fact a grape spirit, correctly called *aguardente* (burning water), distilled from the wines grown in the south of Portugal or the Douro; its production, distribution and price being controlled by a Government body, the Junta Nacional de Aguardente. This spirit, at 77 per cent alcohol by volume, is ready for use soon after distillation. Normally the proportion of *aguardente* to must is 110 litres to 440 litres, constituting a Douro pipe of 550 litres. When a very sweet port or *geropiga* is made, the fermentation is arrested at the earliest opportunity and the *aguardente* would then be increased to 135 litres, while a dry port would take less than the 110 litres.

When port is described as one of the most honest wines in the world, it is a fact that no extraneous substances are added to the wine at any time, other than the natural grape spirit, which in itself is the product of the distilled grape from the country of origin. It is by no means completely neutral in taste and character, and it imparts a special quality to the final product, but when the choice is being made by the tasters before the vintage, they always look for one with a relatively neutral 'nose' and taste.

It seems correct at this point to include reference to an element of non-grape alcohol which appeared in a proportion of the 1972, 1973 and 1974 vintages. This problem came to light only in early 1975. Scientists in Germany had been applying archaeological dating methods to check the age claims for certain ports being sold in that market. Results of these experiments indicated that the port in question was hundreds of years old which was patently not the case. Therefore, the presence of alcohol other than of grape origin was suspected. The problem revolved not around the human consumption of non-grape alcohol (this sort of alcohol is present in many products ingested by our modern society!), but around the legal requirement that only grape alcohol should be used. Alcohol is alcohol, whatever its origins. It is chemically the same and it tastes the same. Only the highly sophisticated liquid scintillation test referred to above can indicate that the carbon atoms in the alcohol were probably not produced by a recently grown grape.

As a matter of fact, in 1904 there was virtually no Portuguese grape spirit available in the country, owing to a very small yield that year, and German spirit (grain or potato) was imported to make the vintage. In the same year a small quantity of *aguardente* was imported by Cockburn Smithes and several other leading shippers from the Azores and other sources, and it is even rumoured that some whisky spirit was imported. A strange twist of fate, that seventy years later the same problems arose, but this time a political issue was made out of them. Strange again that the 1904 was a great year, and those lucky enough to have drunk the famous vintage port of that year will well remember the beauty of that wine.

Bagaceira

After the must has been drawn off from the fermenting tanks, the *bagaço* or solids remain, and these are then removed by hand or automatically, depending upon the fermenting tank and its design, to be put through the hydraulic press. The resultant wine is relatively dry and is normally used for blending purposes at a later stage. When the *bagaço* has been completely pressed it is put into silos where it is kept for a month or two. By then it is completely dry, when it is loaded into a distilling machine where steam is blown through the solids picking up the remaining alcohol, called *bagaceira*. This is a rough white spirit, a kind of *marc*, drunk by the labourers in the vineyards with their coffee in the early hours of the morning, and is usually described as their *mata-bixo* or 'bug-killer'! When reduced in strength and matured in oak casks for some time, the resultant product becomes much smoother and is a popular drink to be found in the cafés, especially in Lisbon.

The lota

After the vintage, the wines are stored in the various types of containers in the Douro *adegas*, where they are allowed to settle for a month or two. In November and December the *lota* takes place: the wines are drawn off their lees, analysed, and examined for strength; extra *aguardente* is added if necessary, as it is possible for a port under 16 per cent alcohol to re-ferment. Normally they are all brought up to a minimum of 19 per cent. The lees are passed through special automatic horizontal presses which extract pure and clean wine from the solids, which is later used for blending in the lower quality ports. However, we are continuously searching for better control and methods of production to maintain the required high qualities of port, so all forms of vinification are continually under review.

The old process of pressing the lees was not only inefficient but in some cases unhygienic. They were placed in canvas sacks, then pressed by large stones being placed on boards on top of these sacks, and very gradually the clean wine would seep through the sacks into troughs and run from these into casks. One must realise, however, that electricity did not become general in the Douro district until a relatively few years ago, and without that modern asset, no modern machinery could be used.

During the months of rest following the vintage, the colour of the red ports seems to fade; then in the following spring the colour returns and increases and the wine seems to *fechar* (close) or bind together again. The wines are then transported down to the maturing lodges in Vila Nova de Gaia.

Maladies which affect port

Before following the wines down to Gaia, we shall mention and analyse some of the various diseases which can attack these fortified wines, and the simple methods of dealing with them.

In theory, if the wine is healthy and carefully produced, the grape in perfect condition, the fermentation controlled and watched, and complete cleanliness and hygiene observed throughout the vintage, there should be no risk of any wine being tainted. However, as we all know, in dealing with Nature it is not always possible to reach perfection. There are fundamentally four bacterial maladies likely to be found in port—*volta* (French, *pousse* or *tourne*; English, tartaric fermentation); *amargo* (French, *vin amer*; English, bitter fermentation); *mannite* (French, *mannite*; English, mannitic fermentation) and *fermentação lactica acetica* (English, lactic acetic fermentation of sugars). A fifth, an enzyme malady called oxidasic casse, must also be included, but this is normally only found in white ports. All these diseases, with the exception of *casse*, are caused by microbes in the ferments and, in certain cases, by chemical changes which, for one reason or another, alter the composition of the wine. These microbes are classified as anaerobic: those that do not develop in contact with the air.

As we have previously noted, the temperature during fermentation is of vital importance. While external temperatures at the vintage can be extremely high, sometimes reaching as much as 45°C, the temperature of the fermenting must should never exceed 32°C. Most microbes start being active above 15°C. The higher the temperature, the greater the increase among these microbes, which can be found in quantities in the atmosphere, the dust, and the vines themselves. The polysaccharides, glucosides and sugars are the substances most subject to alteration and attack.

Volta usually appears, when it appears at all (which is happily very seldom) in the month of April, at the start of the warmer weather. The wine takes on a nutty colour, especially when exposed to the air, as it precipitates the *materia corante* or colouring matter. A simple method of proving the existence of this disease is to fill a small glass tube with the wine. On shaking it well, a silky cloud will form if the disease is present. Wines which are most likely to be affected by this bacteria are those poor in natural acids, and where grapes with mildew have been used. There is a rapid loss of colour and, at the same time, the wines take on a sweet-sour taste with a slight acetic 'nose', reducing the tartaric acids and acidity. The immediate treatment is to add tartaric acids and sulphur dioxide, and finally to pasteurise the wine.

Pousse is similar to *volta*, except that the latter usually only attacks red ports. It forms a gas, which looks like a suspended cloud of steam, producing an unpleasant 'nose' and revealing the carbon dioxide which naturally evolves. The same method of testing is used for this malady, and the wine will show a lack of colour with silky shadows as well as some fizziness. When first examined, a slight 'pricking' will be noticeable on the nose, followed by the smell of acetic ether, and finally, a very flat and neutral aroma. Immediate pasteurisation is essential, and should this prove to be ineffective, the only cure is distillation.

The literal translation of the next malady, *amargo*, is bitter, and self-explanatory. It only affects old red ports, and immediate pasteurisation at 60°C to 72°C for one minute is the sole method of treatment.

The most noticeable symptom of *mannite* is the abnormally large quantity of dry extract and the high content of acid, which is in the form of acetic acid as well as mannitose, and gives the wine a distinctive bitter-sweet flavour. The Portuguese have a name for this malady, *agri–dôce*, bitter-sweet, which describes it perfectly. The bacteria are generally found in wines which are deficient in natural acids, and where high temperatures have been experienced during the fermentation. They develop under these conditions of heat and only appear later, after the vintage. They cannot, however, live in must of high acidity, and pasteurisation at 65°C to 70°C, according to the alcoholic strength, and correction of the acidity, is the only treatment required.

The last malady, *fermentação lactica acetica*, is caused by the presence of various anaerobic bacteria when they attack and destroy the glucose in the wine, forming lactic and acetic acid.

Possibly the most interesting outcome from a three-day study recently with Snr Engenheiro José Viana Marques Gomes, chief of the technical services in the Instituto do Vinho do Porto, was to discover that the two most dreaded diseases mentioned in every previous book on port, the *Mycoderma vini* and *Mycoderma aceti*, cannot attack this wine. This esteemed *engenheiro-agrónomo* refuted this possibility when he delivered a paper at the Colóquio Internacional de Enologia in France in 1973, celebrating the 150th anniversary of the birth of Pasteur. He states that the *Mycoderma vini*, which originates from the microbes which live in contact with the air, rising to the surface of the wine and creating a greyish scum called the *flor do vinho*, or flower, cannot live when the wine exceeds 15 per cent alcohol by volume in strength. As port is a fortified wine and normally the strength is kept at 20 per cent alcohol by volume, neither the *vini* nor the *aceti* can live at this high alcoholic degree.

However, where the wine is fermented in *lagares* or treading tanks, and the *manta*, or solids on the surface, are not continually turned over with the *macacos* or by pumping, these solids can provide perfect breeding grounds for the *mycoderma aceti*, which oxidises the alcohol of the must during the fermentation and forms acetic acid, changing it into vinegar. The small vinegar fly, appropriately called the *Drosophila funebris* or *cellaris*, is always found hovering around any unclean container. It propagates rapidly, laying its eggs on all wine receptacles, and transports the germ from one cask to another. The head of this fly, seen under the microscope, looks like that of an evil horned animal, possibly an appropriate description in every way, as far as the wine man is concerned.

Finally, there are three diseases caused by chemical reaction which, under the heading of *casse*, can be described as brown, blue and white. The first is caused by the inclusion of rotten grapes in the pressing, and it is very simply diagnosed when the wine starts to lose its colour at a very early stage, taking on a brown and rather turbid aspect. To diagnose this malady, pour some of the wine into a glass tube and leave it exposed to the air. If it is a red port, it will take on a most unnatural brick colour and become cloudy. After a few hours it will throw a yellow-brown deposit and its taste will become insipid and slightly bitter. Usually, white ports will react in the same way and become brown in colour. Taken in its early stages, it is fairly simple to correct by adding potassium metabisulphite, forty-eight hours later aerating it violently for two or three hours and then filtering it. The reason for aerating is to oxidize the wine and so destroy the enzyme.

Blue *casse* or *ferrica* appears when the wine comes into contact with iron, which seldom occurs today, with the modern methods of vinification. After leaving wine with this *casse* in contact with the air for some hours, a white, filmy cloud will appear which shows up even more when the wine is swirled around in a glass tube. Within a few days it will then acquire a blue tinge, which is the result of the iron coming into contact with the tannin. The addition of 20 to 75 grammes of tartaric acid per hectolitre, followed by a heavy fining of 100 grammes of gelatine per pipe, will effect a cure.

White *casse* only affects white ports, and cannot really be described as a disease as it is considered to be more of a state of a wine which has been left too long in contact with the air. It takes on a milky colour, and, as in the case of blue *casse*, when spun round the glass tube, will produce a white, milky, spiral cloud. Twenty-five to 30 grammes of citric acid per hectolitre is the cure, followed by a normal fining.

These foregoing maladies are natural ones, which appear every now and then during the production of port, and, although recognised chemists have their own particular formulae for dealing with them, it is probable that those mentioned in this chapter, which have been practised and used over many years of experience, are still the most suitable for the wines of the Douro.

A diversion

An annual event, not directly relevant to port, but one which formerly always followed the vintage, was the partridge shoot. We thought the reader would enjoy a brief insight into the Croft shoot, a highlight of the year.

Together with a few friends, the lodge foreman and some of the office staff, we took the train to Tua where we joined our farmer friend, Antonio Carvalho, his five sons and some 'followers'. On arrival at Ferradoza station, further up the single Douro line, we all disembarked and trekked with our shooting gear, and with guitars flung over our shoulders, down to the river where a Douro boat ferried us across. Horses and mules awaited us there to take us to the Quinta do Arnozelo. This old *adega* or farmhouse, with a large smouldering pile of vine roots in the middle of the stone floor, was our base. Here, the food was cooked in iron cauldrons over the open fire, the smoke finding its own way out through the tiles. An adjoining room was the dormitory where all, except the author and his two British colleagues, slept on the floor. They were accorded two beds, a doubtful honour for the author as it turned out, as he was joined by all the dogs. We had an excellent dinner during which the shoot strategy was discussed. Then early bed was the order of the day.

Five a.m. found us up and dressed enjoying a colossal break-fast comprising cabbage soup, grilled sardines, *bacalhau* (dried codfish), steak, eggs, and heavy country bread, all washed down with wine, port, and coffee, and ultimately, a tot of *bagaceira* all round which sent us clambering up the sheer mountainside at speed. Seven hours later, at an agreed rendezvous, 'hand-maidens' awaited us with a light luncheon. Then onwards, ever onwards, up the steep slopes, and down—wishing one leg had been shorter than the other as it would have made for comfort-able progress—we shot until 5 p.m. At last, laden with par-tridges, back to base.

How welcome was the *adega* that night. A magnificent five-course meal was consumed, helped down by litres of wine and port. This, in turn, brought forth a spate of sentimental speeches, followed by singing accompanied by our guitars. There followed a feeling of close comradeship that none of us was ever likely to forget. A brief three-hour shoot next morning and back to Gaia. Sadly, this shoot was never repeated after the author left Portugal. But we still have our memories.

6

The Lodges in Vila Nova De Gaia

The barco rabelo

No longer do the long and graceful *barcos rabelos* transport the wines from the Douro district to the port entrepôt of Vila Nova de Gaia, lying on the south bank of the river opposite Oporto, the second city of Portugal. Four dams have been nearly completed, from the Spanish frontier to this city, and there are no locks, as yet, to allow boats to complete the journey down the river. Formerly, each spring it was a beautiful sight to see these large flat-bottomed boats carrying their cargo of port, up to fifty or sixty pipes, rowed by men standing at their long oars, and steered by the master on his bridge.

At that time, the river was swollen with the winter rains and melting snows from the mountains in Spain, and the fast currents helped them with their arduous and sometimes dangerous voyage. Only the captain's complete knowledge of the river, with its swirling rapids and whirlpools, made it navigable and enabled the boats to arrive at their destination intact. He was usually the owner of the boat, and had to hold a special river-master's ticket, which was checked regularly by the authorities. The crew lived, ate and slept on board, but as it is not permitted to navigate at night, the boat was always tied up after dark.

The boat was unique and it is sad that it is now becoming extinct. Its origin is fascinating: although it had been used purely as a river-boat in the Douro for over a thousand years, the crew were still called *marinheiros* (sailors) and the captain the *maater*. When the Vikings sailed their long warships from

Scandinavia to the Mediterranean in the mid-ninth century, some of their ships were wrecked on the Portuguese coast, a dangerous one at any time. Others landed to take on food and stores, and the Portuguese, being a seafaring nation, studied the boats and copied them for their own use. (Some people say that these boats appeared even earlier, during the Roman ages, but there is no evidence of this).

The clinker-built Viking boats were constructed for the open seas, and their sails and rudders, being small, were of little use in the river; so the Portuguese increased the size of the sails, lengthened the rudder, and broadened the beam. They still found them difficult to manoeuvre in the river, and again increased the size of the sail and rudder. Having done this, they found it necessary to build a bridge, aft of the huge sail, as the length of the rudder had become unmanageable, and the bottom of the sail had also to be hitched up to give clear forward vision. So at last they served their purpose as reliable river-boats.

Being flat-bottomed, the boat draws very little water, and is usually built from well-seasoned chestnut, with a superstructure of pine. The hull is liberally covered with goat fat and the stern and bow painted with various bright colours. The length of some of the larger boats is as much as fifteen metres or even more, and it is a fascinating sight to see the national *bacalhau*, garlic strings, smoked hams and sausages of various shapes and sizes hanging up on the trellised bridge, which is also used as the store-cupboard. The cooking is done in a black iron pot over an open charcoal fire on board, and a small cask of table wine is stored aft, in the cool of the stern.

Happily the prevailing winds in the winter and spring are south-westerly, which enables the boats to be sailed upriver. The journey can take up to seven or eight days, as on reaching the upper stretches of the river, the crew have to land, and literally pull the boat up with ropes. In some places where the rapids were too strong even for the men, teams of oxen would await them to haul them up.

The loading of the full casks at the river's edge was always a rowdy affair. These were usually brought down by ox-cart, and then rolled to the boat by four or five men. Ropes were used to drag them on board and lever them into position, stacking them three high. Samples were taken from each cask, sealed and sent down to the lodges in Vila Nova de Gaia, in order to compare them with the wine when it eventually arrived, as it had been known occasionally to have 'altered' slightly, due to some 'human absorption' during the journey downriver!

This is now all past history, as the port is transported down either by rail or transporter lorries, and three last remaining *barcos rabelos* lie in the river at Vila Nova de Gaia, moored alongside the shore, as a reminder of the good old days.

The lodges

The word 'lodge' originates from the Portuguese *loja*, meaning a storehouse, shop or cellar, and these red-tiled cool buildings can be seen stretching their way up the steep sides of Vila Nova de Gaia. Here the new wines, which have had time to settle in the Douro during the autumn and winter months, will spend years maturing in the many thousands of vats and casks.

Up to the time of the Russian occupation of the Baltic countries, casks of oak mostly from Memel and Stettin were used for ageing the wines, but since the imports from these countries ceased, other woods have been used. New Orleans oak was found to give a strong taste to the wines, even after the normal six-month period of seasoning with young wines; Italian chestnut was considered inferior in quality, and Persian oak, apart from being exceedingly expensive, was rather porous. So today, Portuguese oak and chestnut are almost exclusively used for casks. Oak is a very hard wood and difficult to work, but it is strong and long-lasting, which is as well, for national oak is becoming scarcer and more difficult to obtain and we have to penetrate deeper and deeper into the mountainous regions of Portugal to find it.

The chestnut casks are normally used for shipping, but not for maturing port, and after the normal seasoning, they are treated with a liquid paraffin which neutralises them.

Apart from these casks, large vats are also used for maturing port; these are normally made from *macacauba* (Brazilian mahogany), but with the present-day shortage and cost of the wood, cement vats have now been introduced into the lodges for blending purposes and short-term storage. These latter containers slow down the maturing process as the wines cannot breathe as they do through wood, and are virtually 'bottled', but obviously they are more convenient for blending and general work in the lodge. The large mahogany vats stand on cement or granite supports, unpainted, showing off their natural beauty and the colour of the wood. Generally at least two-thirds of the total stock of port in the lodges is stored in wood.

Cooperage

Up to a few years ago, virtually all port was shipped to the four corners of the world in casks of specific sizes, namely shipping pipes, hogsheads, quarter-casks and, occasionally octaves (eighths) and sixteenths. As wood became scarcer and more expensive, large 2,500-litre metal containers were used, and these, today, are the usual method of shipping in bulk. At the same time, modern marketing and brand building is increasing world-wide, and today over one-third of port shipped is bottled in the shippers' lodges.

Following the introduction of metal containers and cement vats, there are far fewer coopers than there used to be. It is sad that the art of cooperage is fast disappearing, as this art has always been passed on from father to son from one generation to the next, and anything attached to family traditions is good and, one hopes, enduring. However, though the freight and transport costs of a metal container are cheaper than those of casks, the latter are still shipped to smaller customers, mostly in Europe. It must be said that the metal container is an excellent method of transporting port as most of these are constructed in stainless steel which in no way can affect or damage the wine. And further, they are far stronger than casks, which have been known to be dropped occasionally, causing problems to the insurance companies as well as the customer, who possibly needed the wine at that moment.

How is a cask made? To begin with, the formation of the staves and the head is all-important, and after that the hoops to bind them together. But every stage needs precision. Anyone interested in wine must know about wood, in which wine matures. I feel that we should take the construction of a shipping pipe, step by step from its first inception to the finished result.

When the oak tree has been felled and transported to the cooperage, it is cut into the right lengths and widths, then left out in the open to dry and season for at least two years, after which time any bad wood is obvious and is separated from the good. Approximately thirty-seven staves are necessary to make up a pipe, and these are shaped by machine, the ends being narrower than the middles. The new staves are placed horizontally on a long plank with various notches denoting the final size of the cask to be made, and this is used as the measure. The cooper next fits these staves together, upstanding, within one hoop at the top to hold them temporarily. When they are all assembled, he adds more hoops to keep them in position. A chain is then placed around the bottom end of the future cask, and this is attached to a handle; a fire is lit inside the cask, and the wood dampened with water. When the wood is sufficiently hot, the handle is turned, slowly tightening the chain and bringing the bottoms of the formed staves together. When these have closed completely, another hoop is rapidly placed over them and knocked down firmly, followed by other hoops.

The cask is now allowed to cool, the heads are inserted and the new shipping pipe is ready for measuring. To measure the cask, it is filled with water, which is then emptied into a measuring tank, and should the final measurement not be exact, the size is adjusted by changing a stave for a wider or narrower one, as necessary.

The cask has twelve hoops and each hoop has its own particular name and use: the *mola, javre, colete, rabo de palha, sobre bojo, bojo*. Each name has its own significance: for instance *rabo de palha* means 'tail of the reed', denoting the hoop which is situated at the end of a length of reed which is inserted between the end of the staves to prevent any leakage. The heads are also named: the one with the bung is called the *fundo de duas aranhas*, the head, or base, with two scratches, while the opposite is the *fundo de uma aranha* (one scratch). The head planks are also named: *xintel*, *peça* and *mião*. After the cask is made and measured, it is washed out with an alkaline solution and filled with a young wine for seasoning, which normally takes about six months.

When shipping casks are returned after use, they must, by law, be broken down, examined, repaired if necessary, and then re-built.

Some forty tools and implements are used daily in the art of coopering, and many have romantic names in Portuguese; but they lose much in the translation. You find the *gibardoira de pipa*, grooved cutters for the eventual insertion of the head, *trado de batoque*, the bung borer, and the *barbequim*, a large crooked gimlet. One hopes that all these old tools will go on being used, as this art comes from many thousands of years of experience and practice and should not ever be allowed to die.

The following are the various types of casks used in the lodge for maturing wines, or shipping, with their respective contents in litres:

Lodge lot cask for maturing	=	about 630 litres
Douro casks	=	550 litres
Shipping pipes	=	534·24 litres
Hogsheads	=	267 litres
Quarter-casks	=	134 litres

Octaves and sixteenths of a pipe are virtually never used today, as the wine will rapidly acquire a 'woody nose' caused by the relatively high proportion of wood to wine.

An amusing incident happened to me when giving a lecture on port in Amsterdam a few years ago in a very old hall, equivalent to one of the English City Halls. While I was showing a slide on the old cooperage tools used in Gaia, a member of the audience interrupted the lecture by remarking that the large tapestry hanging at the end of the hall happened to include every one of these tools, and this tapestry was dated 1385!

Maturing and blending

Now to the story of the young wines arriving from the Douro valley. It is usual for the shipper to purchase his wines from the same vineyards year after year in order to maintain the continuity and style of the wines of the House. There has already been a first classification of the wines immediately after the actual vintage, and during the months when they are resting in the Douro. On arrival in Gaia, every pipe is re-examined in the tasting room and in the laboratory; the tasters then proceed to give them their final destination.

Each wine will be given a name and number, the former being the district or *quinta* with the date of the vintage and the latter a lot number referring to the lot sheet, which will contain the complete record of the wine for the rest of its life. It will record the quantity, whether red or white, dry or sweet, the strength, sweetness in degrees Baumé, and the complete analytical history. The mark and number of the lot sheet will then be transferred on to each cask-head, and these casks will be kept together in the lodges, maturing until they are required for blending and shipping.

The taster will know, from his experience and the knowledge of his stocks, for which brand the wine will eventually be used, and he can judge whether the wine itself will stand up to ten, twenty or many more years of maturing, or whether it will be necessary to use it in a younger and less expensive blend. It is the taster's duty to watch the wines during their lives in casks and to note any changes. The principal thing to remember is that all port is matured in casks, and eventually blended for shipping brands, except for vintage port, which will be dealt with separately.

It is natural for all red ports gradually to lose their colour during maturation, some quicker than others depending upon the original quality, the grape variety, and the weather conditions of the year. White ports, on the other hand, gain colour in wood through oxidation. The young and healthy red port, on arrival from the Douro, should be blue–purple in colour, full and fruity in body, and fresh and eager on the taste and nose. In fact, it can be so dark that the taster's teeth and tongue will become discoloured after tasting many of these young wines. Gradually this purple wine will change to red, with a brown hue, continuing to lose some of its depth of colour. Eventually, after many years in cask, it will attain a tawny colour, becoming paler and paler as the years pass. The taste and nose will obviously relate itself to the age. This simple process really defines the three main wood ports in a nutshell—ruby, tawny and white. The first, ruby, is a young wine, dark ruby in colour which matures and becomes gradually tawny with age, turning into the second type. The third is a port made from white grapes.

Naturally, these three very distinct styles of port can be subdivided into many varieties: some lighter, some darker, some sweeter, some drier. Included among the rubies is 'vintage character', which is a full-bodied wine and a blend of fine years, mellow, with some characteristics of a vintage port, but matured in wood, not in bottle, as is the latter.

The tawnies and old tawnies are lighter in style and more aromatic and delicate than the rubies, owing to their long life in wood. However, by their very nature they must be a more expensive wine, and should the consumer prefer this style of port, but be unable to afford it, he can obtain a young tawny, which is a blend of red and white port, both young and sound, and producing a lighter product than a young ruby. This blend does not have the bouquet and taste of an older tawny, but it is quite acceptable, and satisfies the demand for a wine of that style at a more reasonable price.

The white ports can be divided into two categories, the medium sweet, having a light and pleasant flavour, and popular in Sweden and France, and the very dry apéritif port, which is served before meals in Portugal. It is a revelation to those who imagine that port is only red, sweet and heavy.

The way to determine the age of red port is to hold the glass at an angle against a white background, when you will see the colour of the rim of the wine—bluish-purple when very young, gradually becoming browner with age, and eventually a yellowy-greenish tinge when exceedingly old. The young tawny will have a definite pink-coloured rim against the true yellow tawny of the old one.

In its natural life-cycle, all wine throws a deposit while maturing, and the younger and fuller the wine, the heavier the deposit. A wood port should always be fresh and alive, and that is the reason why these wines are racked off their deposit or lees

every year to maintain this freshness. At the same time they are tested for strength and tasted. By racking them they are automatically aerated, as this entails transferring them by electric pumps from the casks to large vats, great care being taken not to disturb the lees at the bottom of the casks. Technically, lees in young ports are produced by micro-organisms, yeasts, bacteria, tartrates, *materia corante* (colouring matters) and other substances which are precipitated by the action of the alcohol, and also by the effect of low and high temperatures and of aeration.

The lees in old and mature ports are effected mostly by the precipitation of the *materia corante*. Sometimes something similar to a very large watering-can 'rose' is fitted to the tap at the base of the vat; the wine pours through this into an open wooden trough and is then pumped back again into the top of the vat. This continues for a few hours, thoroughly aerating the wine. The lees are removed from the casks and passed through special hydraulic filters and the resultant clean wine, *prensas*, is blended into the cheaper brands.

When the wines become older and lighter in colour and more delicate, they throw far less deposit, and ten-year-old and older wines are normally racked every eighteen months. The very ancient twenty- and thirty-year-olds are treated with the respect they deserve, and even today we still find some lodges using the old method of aerating these wines by the lodgeman, who uses an *almude* (a measure, 21 *almudes* = 1 pipe) balanced on his head to give the treatment to this precious liquid, and then returns it to the cask. This also gives the coopers the opportunity of examining the lot casks and repairing them when necessary.

The blending stage is the most important operation of all in the port taster's work, as it is he who has to produce a wine, shipped usually under a registered brand, that must be identical in every respect to the last one shipped, in order that the consumer is always satisfied. This brand must maintain the continuity of its style, age, sweetness, colour, strength, 'nose' and taste.

Whatever method is used, a shipping blend sheet must be compiled, stating the various wines of different ages necessary to make up the final blend and brand, whose character must compare absolutely with the last shipping sample. This sounds as if it could be quite a simple operation, but one must not forget that although the wines from the same *quintas* or districts are normally used in the blend so as to maintain the style and type of the brand, every year the wines vary in colour, sweetness and taste and no wines are identical from one vintage to the other. For instance the 1948 vintage was one of the hottest for many decades, external temperatures rising to 45°C, and a great proportion of the crop was burned. The resultant must was very dark, full-bodied and sweet. In 1949 the weather was cooler and rather wet and the musts were thin, light in colour and dry. The following year the weather was perfect and the 1950 vintage was generally declared by all shippers. This was, and still is, a beautifully balanced wine. These are examples of three consecutive years when the wines produced were completely different one from the other. So, basically, when making up a blend, and knowing the wines maturing in the lodges, the differences or variations must be compensated by blending into the shipping lot a sweeter, drier, darker or lighter wine to balance these differences.

Before we go any further, it should be explained that a pipe of port is divided into twenty-one *almudes* or two hundred and fifty-two *canadas*, and these are the measures used when making up a blend. One *almude* is 25·44 litres and one *canada* is 2·12 litres. When the age of port is mentioned or printed on the label (age, *not* date) it means the average age. For instance, a port 'aged in wood for ten years' means that there is probably a proportion of that wine in that blend far older than ten years, but there is also some younger wine. It is the final blend and average age that counts. This is an important point to remember, as no old tawny has any mention of a date.

The taster sends his list of samples to be drawn straight from the casks in the lodges and proceeds to make up his blend in a glass measure marked in *almudes* and *canadas*. Normally there are 'back-up' lots for the old tawny brands, as the finest young wines at the vintage are reserved and later blended together to mature for this purpose. Although this method has no similarity to the sherry *solera* system, the effect is not dissimilar. However, the young tawnies are quite different: blends of young rubies and white ports, averaging from four to six years. As much as six to eight *almudes* per pipe of white could be used in a blend to counteract the full-bodied young rubies; again, this would depend upon the colour of the red ports of the year. Both the rubies and the young tawnies are normally termed as 'commercial' wines which, actually, is a most uncomplimentary description.

To blend a vintage character port can be more of a problem as normally the wines in this blend are all Cima Corgo wines of

E   129

good years and it is difficult for the shipper to determine which of his ultimate stock of first-class wines should be reserved for vintage port, old tawnies or vintage character. So the wines used must certainly be from the Cima Corgo but not necessarily from vintage years. Although vintage years only occur occasionally when the farmer is blessed by perfect weather conditions throughout the year, some excellent wines are made every year, again through the influence of the Douro microclimates. These are the type of wines generally used in the vintage character and crusted port blends.

Finally, before shipment the colour is registered in a tintometer, the Baumé measurement or sweetness is taken, and the strength assessed by distillation; but the vital assessment—the taste and the 'nose'—can only be made by the taster.

Vintage port is undoubtedly the greatest of all ports. This wine represents only 2 per cent of the annual shipments of port to the world. It takes two years, that is, two winters and a summer, before the shipper can be absolutely sure of the final quality of the wine to which he will attach his name and on which the reputation of his House will depend. Only then will he know how the wine is developing and whether it will stand ten, fifteen, twenty or more years maturing in bottle.

This wine, of one superb year, is a blend of wines from the best vineyards. Every shipper knows, more or less, where his competitor is buying his wines at the vintage, but he does not know the actual blends in his vintage port. What he does know, however, is that, basically, the wine is from his own vineyard which gives it the style and type of his House. Therefore we can only describe the blend of a Croft vintage port when we say that between twelve and fourteen *almudes* of our *quinta da Roêda* is used in the blend (a very aromatic and mature wine), while the nine or seven *almudes* making up the balance of the pipe will come from other first-class Cima Corgo farmers of relatively 'greener' wines to counteract this maturity. We shall never forget Mr Frank Yeatman's (Taylor, Fladgate and Yeatman) remarks on vintage port: 'A little bit of "green", my boy, is necessary to produce the "grip".' If any reader has had the privilege of drinking Taylor's 1912, he will know what this venerable gentleman meant by this remark.

In simple arithmetic, a blend of half a fifteen-year-old and half a five-year-old would produce an average ten-year-old tawny. But this is certainly not the case, as the proportion of the five-year-old would 'kill' the fifteen-year-old by its relative youth, roughness, and deeper colour. The art of blending port is far more complicated than this. Possibly the best method of demonstrating the taster's problem is actually to show a blend of a ten-year-old made up in 1976, in the 21 *almudes* measure equivalent to one pipe.

		almudes	*canadas*
VT 1967		1	6
	VT 1966	1	6
VT 1964/5		3	8
	VT 1965	7	1
VT 1963/4		2	10
	VT 1969	2	2
VT 1968		1	5
	VT seco 1964	0	9
AD		0	1
TOTAL		21	0

We feel that a more detailed description of the various blends is now necessary to enlighten the reader. VT means *vinho tinto*, or red port; 1964/5, for instance, means a blend of these two years which are first-class wines reserved for this brand; *seco* means dry, as the final blend was found to be a trifle sweet in comparison with the last shipment; and AD is *aguardente* or grape spirit, which was necessary to include to bring the wine up to shipping strength. All these wines in the blend would obviously be produced from the best vineyards in the Cima Corgo.

Even today a shipper is sometimes called upon by his customer to match a wine from a competitor. The shipper will have

to delve deeply into his 'library' of stock to find the wines which could match the style of this wine, and eventually produce the desired quality. His stock position must always come into the final decision, as, should the wine be a ten-year-old tawny, it must never be forgotten that to ship, say, two hundred pipes of this wine per annum, the shipper has to hold a stock of at least two thousand pipes. The cost of this investment alone is astronomical!

Should the final blend be too sweet, one of the wines used in the blend being the culprit, a dry wine is then added to bring down the level of the sugar content. Conversely, a *geropiga*, or very sweet port, either white or red, would be used to raise sweetness. As much as two to three *almudes* per pipe of the latter could be used in the blend. Sometimes, the addition of *aguardente* is necessary before shipment to raise the shipping strength to 20 per cent alcohol by volume. One *canada* per pipe of this grape alcohol at 77 per cent alcohol by volume will increase the strength by 0·2 per cent.

As for very large 'commercial' wine lots and blends, it is always advantageous to blend these well ahead of shipping as the many wines used in the blend will be given the opportunity of 'marrying' and settling down. Here we are talking of lots of one hundred or more pipes which will include anything up to twenty or thirty various wines of different years, mostly relatively young. When we say 'ahead', this would mean at least a year or eighteen months.

Official description of types

Sadly, in the past, dates have been bandied about on wines which had little or no similarity to vintage ports or wines of one year, so now the Instituto do Vinho do Porto has issued official regulations governing the description of ports, with dates and indication of age. A résumé of this official document is as follows:

Vintage: a port of one harvest, produced in a year of recognised quality, with exceptional organoleptic characteristics, dark and full bodied, with very fine aroma and palate, and which is recognised by the Instituto do Vinho do Porto as having the right to the description 'vintage' and corresponding date. It must comply with the following regulations: to obtain approval of the description 'vintage', (a) a sample of the wine should be submitted to the I.V.P. between 1st January and 30th September of the second year counting from the year of the harvest; (b) the stock of this port must be declared at the time approval is requested, and an account showing sales will be opened; (c) the bottling of the approved wine should be between 1st July of the second year and 30th June of the third year, counting from the year of the harvest, preferably the classic dark-coloured glass bottle should be used and the I.V.P. must be informed of the date of bottling this wine and two reference samples must be submitted; (d) the wine must be sold exclusively in bottle, bearing the *selo de garantia* (seal of guarantee), and the approval of the I.V.P. must be obtained for the labels and presentation; (e) the main label should indicate clearly the shipper or brand, the year of the vintage and the description 'vintage' quite apart from any other supplementary details which may also be approved; (f) while this regulation essentially safeguards the word 'vintage', the descriptions *tipo vintage, vintage style, vintage character* or similar approved translations are permitted on labels or publicity material, but it is expressly forbidden to mention dates or to make any other reference which could cause confusion with genuine vintage, and even these descriptions are permitted only for wines whose organoleptic qualities justify them; (g) it is expressly forbidden to use the word 'vintage' accompanied by the date of the harvest for any other ports, and particularly not for late-bottled vintage or L.B.V.

Late-bottled vintage, or L.B.V., is again a port of one year of good quality, bearing the high standards required to be approved by the I.V.P., but in this case the bottling should take place between 1st July of the fourth year and 31st December of the sixth year counting from the year of the harvest. The same regulations apply as for vintage except that the main label should indicate the year of bottling as well as the vintage, and the description 'late-bottled vintage' or 'L.B.V.' must appear on one line only and be printed in the same type and colour.

The last of the dated wines, *port wine with the date of harvest*, is certainly not intended to be taken as a vintage port, nor is it a late-bottled vintage as it cannot be bottled before it is seven years old, and in this way tends to be more towards a tawny in character. Samples of wine intended to be sold in this way have to be submitted between 1st July and 31st December of the third year following the harvest, but wines acquired direct from the farmers or the Casa do Douro can be submitted at any time for the appreciation of the I.V.P. The sale of these wines must be made exclusively in bottle under the *selo de garantia* and are subject to the approval of the respective labels. They are normally sold immediately after bottling and there is a special provision for re-assessment if they spend long in bottle before sale. Apart from Garrafeira (which are ports often sold in Portugal that have had a substantial period in bottle) those that are sold immediately on bottling can also add the descriptions *reserva, reserve, House reserve* or some similar approved name. The label must include the information that the wine has been aged in casks. Otherwise the general regulations as to approval, accounts, labelling, and so on, follow the same general outline as with the two previous wines.

The fourth wine to be mentioned in this official document is *port with an indication of age*, but no date. The four indicated ages permitted to be used are, 10 years old, 20 years old, 30 years old and over 40 years old. The sales must be made exclusively in bottle and the indication of the age, and that the wine has been matured in wood, must be shown on the main label, while the year of bottling may be shown either on the main or back label.

Age and vintages

In 1945, on the author's return to Portugal after the war, an amusing incident occurred relevant to dated wines. During the vintage, on visiting one of the many *quintas*, he was greeted by an old farmer friend who happened to be a great Anglophile, and he was immediately offered a special bottle of port which had been kept for the occasion. The farmer proudly declared that this was 'at least a hundred years old'. With great ceremony the bottle was opened and the author noticed that the cork seemed to be a trifle clean and young for a bottle of wine of that age. The port was very pale and yellow in colour, but the real surprise came when it was 'nosed' and tasted. Unexpected brandy fumes nearly knocked him over and the taste was enough to cause him to extinguish his cigarette and rush for a glass of water.

On enquiring from the farmer why the wine happened to be 'rather strong', he was informed that this was the last bottle of a port bottled by his grandfather from their own *quinta*. Through-out the years the port had been regularly opened and topped up with *aguardente* at 77 per cent alcohol by volume, this because they assumed that any wine, after a long period of time in bottle, would lose strength. In fact, the port had been converted into what amounted to almost neat brandy. Not wishing to insult the kindly farmer, we sat down together and steadily finished the bottle. History does not relate the results of this experience!

The aforementioned official rules are important, but they concern only a very small percentage of the port trade; vintage port, for instance, accounts for a mere 2 per cent. It has already been mentioned that this wine only appears on an aver-age every three or four years, and sometimes even less often, so the natural question is: 'Why does the shipper not make a much larger quantity when a vintage is declared?' It certainly would be a great asset if this were possible, but it must be remembered that old tawnies, developing and maturing in cask for many years, must also have the quality and backing from these first-class wines, as a lower-quality ruby will not develop into a first-class old tawny simply by keeping it for twenty or more years.

When bottling vintage port, the choice of the cork and the bottle is all-important, as the former should be longer than normal, close-grained, and completely clean and white at one end with no flaws to contaminate the wine. Preferably the bottle should be as dark as possible to enable the wine to mature slowly, thus storing up inside the exquisite bouquet and taste, only to be released on opening and decanting. Decanting, dealt with in more detail later on, is always necessary because of the wine throwing its natural lees, which eventually, after many years, will harden and become the crust.

Contrary to general belief, very old tawnies do not normally improve in bottle, as their natural life is in cask. The bottle, in this case, is merely a method of transporting the old wine from the cask to the glass, and the fresher the wine is, the better, though some people think that a short rest of a month or two after the bottle has travelled to the cellar improves the wine.

Some time ago a very popular style of port was found in most of the clubs in London. It was called 'crusting port', and was a blend of two or three years of first-class wines, matured in cask for three or four years, and then bottled. This wine, being full-bodied, would naturally throw a crust after some years in bottle, and the advantage was the possibility of drinking it much earlier than the vintage port. This is now being generally replaced by the late-bottled vintage, as crusting port cannot, by law, show a vintage date.

When a shipper declares a vintage he normally thinks of fifteen years ahead as, purely from experience, this is generally the time when the wine begins to show its real qualities. However, it is impossible to lay down any rules as to when the wine will be at its best, or when it will start to 'go over the top'. At the time of writing the 1945s, 1947s, 1955s and 1960s, for instance, are drinking well, but in the same breath one can add that so are the 1912s, 1917s, 1920s, 1927s and other fifty- and sixty-year-old vintage ports (if they are to be found!).

A true story will help to illustrate the problem of laying down rules. When, in 1965, the 1963s were being shown, we visited a well-known purchasing director of a famous group of hotels in London, who bought ten pipes of our vintage port to lay down for the future. When he was asked what year they were serving in the restaurants at that time his reply was the 1955s. We were rather surprised that this first-class hotel should be showing a ten-year-old vintage, as we considered it to be far too young. The director smiled in a friendly fashion at our startled expressions and said: 'I always keep our 1937 wine list to show you pompous shippers that in that year we were serving the 1927s!' And the stocks of vintage ports at that time were far greater than they were in 1965.

So, in the end, who are we, the 'pompous shippers' to tell the consumers their taste? We can only humbly advise. As a rough guide we generally suggest twenty years for a first-rate vintage, fifteen for a lighter vintage, and well over twenty years for a superb vintage.

Possibly it would be wiser to discuss only the post-Second

World War vintages and their merits because pre-war vintage ports are very rare, virtually non-commercial, and extremely difficult to find today. In Appendix I, you will find a complete list of vintages and their shippers from 1869 to the present day, but time and space do not permit a detailed account of each wine and the reason why they were declared and shipped. Including the 1945s, there have been seventeen vintages shipped to date, but by the figures denoting the shippers of the year, the 'general' vintage year will be simple to find.

Year	Number of shippers declared
1945	25
1947	14
1948	10
1950	16
1951	1
1952	2
1954	3
1955	28
1957	2
1958	14
1960	27
1962	1
1963	25
1966	21
1967	7
1970	39

In fact, there have only been seven 'general' years since 1945. This latter vintage was a post-war 'gift from heaven' as relatively few vintages had been declared since 1935, but, unfortunately, it was only a small vintage in quantity owing to post-war economical factors. Virtually all this wine was bottled in Oporto as port was then on a quota to the United Kingdom, which lasted until 1949, and this naturally inhibited any shipper from shipping wine for laying down as they needed a quick turnover on their huge investments in stocks, and the answer to this lay in wood ports. So the 1945 vintage was really the first time ever that a vintage port was wholly bottled in Portugal and not in the United Kingdom, remembering always that 98 per cent of this wine was drunk in Britain. Anyone having the good fortune of possessing a few bottles of this wine will appreciate the beauty and splendour of the year even after thirty-odd years in bottle, and will realise that the wine still has a long way to go before its decline.

The 1947s were lighter and more delicate than the 1945s, and because of the small quantities declared, have possibly all been drunk by now.

The 1948 was one of the hottest vintages for many years and temperatures rose to 45°C. The crop was relatively small, owing to the grapes being burned on the vines, but the *quintas* facing the east and lying on the south bank of the river gained considerably by their geographical position. The wine was very sweet, very full-bodied and will last for many years. In some of the wines one can detect a slight 'burnt' nose, which certainly does not detract from the quality.

The 1950s were completely different from the 1948s. Gentle and delicate at birth, they have been described as the 'lady's' vintage. Originally they were thought to be short-livers, but, as the female sex tends to outlive the male, so does this wine continue to live and improve. Not a '45 nor a '48, but hopefully they will see us through another decade.

Feuerheerd was the only shipper of 1951 and Kopke and Mackenzie of 1952, and three shippers declared the 1954: Burmester, Mackenzie and Offley Forrester. When asked why should only these few shippers declare these three years, we must remind you that some excellent wines are made every year, and these shippers' *quintas* and districts where they made their wine were obviously blessed by the microclimates of the region. No shipper would declare a vintage which was not worthy of the prestige of their name.

Happily 1955 produced another 'general' vintage and diminishing stocks of this type of wine were again replenished. This was a good all-round year producing well-balanced wines, full-bodied and fruity, and even now after twenty years they are drinking well and still have some time to go.

Though only Mackenzie and Butler and Nephew declared the 1957, fourteen shippers shipped the 1958s. This latter year was fairly wet on the whole but some excellent wines were made. Most shippers declared the 1960 vintage, a very good and well-balanced wine. The actual date of the start of the vintage was very early, generally on 12th September, as the month was extremely hot. However, slight rain fell during the picking, which cooled the temperatures of the musts, and most farmers were pleased with the early start as rain fell nearly every day after the 24th of the month.

Undoubtedly 1963 was a very great year both in quantity and quality, and the wine was declared by most shippers. The harvesting period was held under ideal conditions: hot days and cool nights, and the slight rainfall which occurred just prior to the general date of starting, 22nd September, softened the skins and filled the grapes.

Though rain heralded 1966, none fell between April and September except for a very light shower just before the start of the vintage. The drought, however, caused a drop in the yield as the grapes were small, and many were dry. This produced high sugar contents and though rain began to fall on the 26th September, this could only be beneficial in every way, and the sugar contents continued to remain high.

A very cold start to 1967, when temperatures remained below zero for some time, produced a late and small flowering in the spring. Heavy thunderstorms did not improve the situation and maturation of this small yield was slow. However, some excellent wines were produced and seven shippers declared their wine as vintages—Cockburn Smithes, Gonzalez Byass, Martinez Gassiot, Offley Forrester, Manuel Poças, Sandeman, and Taylor. Croft declared their single *quinta da Roêda* 1967, the first since 1868.

The weather in 1970 was virtually perfect for the maturation of the grapes—heavy rainfall in the first two months, cold but dry in March, a very warm April for the flowering, followed by a hot spring and summer. A short period of rain at the beginning of September producing perfect picking conditions for the start of the vintage on the 21st. Extraordinarily high external temperatures of 46°C were reached during this month, which produced more mature wines, and these are now softer than the 1966s, but nevertheless a good follow-on. This vintage was generally shipped by all shippers.

Since then only Dows declared the 1972 and we, the shippers, all await our next 'gift'. May it come quickly!

Although the pre-*phylloxera* vintages were undoubtedly 'fatter' and more full-bodied, it does not mean their quality was any better than the post-*phylloxera* ones, as early 'beef and brawn' need not necessarily indicate the final quality.

Tasting

Despite the ever-increasing involvement by the wine chemist in the production of wine, it is still the taster who has the final word, which is, of course, the key to the secret and the continuity of our wine. Only many years of experience, close association with and love of wine can teach anyone the art of tasting. There are some who have a natural talent and a gift for this, women often being among their number. In fact, the firms of Guimaraens and Wiese & Krohn have both at different times had a woman as their chief taster, each of these very highly considered in their profession.

To describe the art of tasting is almost impossible, as no mere words can possibly portray the infinite subtleties of the palate and olfactory senses when judging and selecting the many different types of ports of varying ages and their qualities which make up the final blends. The sensation of tasting is a very personal and elusive thing. To try and convey to someone else exactly what it is you taste in a wine is a difficult feat. 'This wine is sweet,' you will say, and that is simple. 'It is round and full,' you add, but these are shapes, not tastes. 'It is fruity,' you try to explain, but fruitiness is surely a matter of smell rather than taste. The actual sensations of taste are said to be four: sweetness, bitterness, sourness and saltiness, while some experts add, tentatively, alkaline and metallic tastes. All tastes are some combination of these basic half-dozen. Indeed, an experienced taster hardly tastes at all, in the strict sense of the word, as practically all his work is done on the nose, and the palate only confirms what his nose has already told him.

As to the actual procedure of tasting, there is nothing to equal the experience you yourself gain by practice. What we can endeavour to do is to suggest how to make the best use of such opportunities of tasting wines which may come your way. One should always taste against a standard set in one's own mind. 'I like this,' you may say of a wine, 'it reminds me of a '45 I tasted last month, but it seems to be sweeter (or less round, or not quite as fruity, etc).' You have begun to assemble your wine memory or library, which you will add to with every wine you taste critically in the future. It is an amusing fact that many tasters with years of experience will automatically raise their glasses to their noses before drinking at table, even should the liquid be water—which is seldom the case!

Moving to the tasting-room, we find the correct tasting-glass —a narrow tulip-shaped one with a short stem. Meticulously washed and never dried with a cloth which could affect the final 'nose', it is sparkling and odourless. Wiping the lip of the bottle, and filling the glass about a third full, will enable you to swill the wine around, allowing it to mix with the air. First look at the colour of the wine, to see that it is bright and clear, and then follow that by examining the edge or rim of the wine, which will give you some indication of the age. As we have already mentioned, a purple-blue colour will indicate youth, and as the age increases this becomes browner and eventually, with great age, hardly red at all but rather brown with a slight yellow-green tinge.

The swirling of the wine will have released the 'ethers', and so, gradually bringing the glass up to the nose until this is deep in the glass, the full bouquet can be analysed. When 'nosing' the wine, all your senses must be concentrated on pinpointing every aspect of the aroma and assessing exactly what you personally find. Be blind and deaf to all exterior distractions for these few moments, and try to place exactly the sensations which the wine conveys to you.

You then ask yourself: is the wine clean with no unpleasant undertones? Does it suggest sweetness or acidity, fruitiness or floweriness? Does it perhaps remind you of the gum cistus wild rose in the Douro valley in the spring? Try to identify each fragrant and delicate sense which floats before you, and store this away in your mental library. By experience, you learn the various unpleasant smells of diseased wines such as those with high acidity, mildew, and non-vinous smells caused by dirty casks and vats, as well as the normal ones such as 'greeness' or youth, maturity, wood and all the various ones that crop up from day to day. When you have made up your mind about the 'nose' then physically taste the wine.

First, retain it in your mouth, rolling it round and swilling it against the palate over the tongue. At the same time, through drawn lips, suck in a little air so that it hisses slightly as it meets and mixes with the wine in your mouth. This air is necessary in order to allow the wine to give up its flavours and ethers to your taste buds. You then obtain all the sensations the wine is able to produce—its sweetness, roundness and completeness. Only then should the wine be spat out; that is of course, if you are in the tasting-room and not at table!

Undoubtedly, the most important factor in tasting is complete honesty. You must be honest with yourself and taste with a completely open mind, to reach an honest opinion. You must stick to your final judgement, whether right or wrong. Opinions are always very personal when tasting, but the great word—humility—must never be forgotten, as over the centuries even the world's greatest tasters have admitted that they are liable to error. Everyone is human! A retentive memory is essential to a professional taster, but in the case of vintage ports this memory can only depend upon the opportunity of drinking the various wines, and remembering their years and respective qualities and peculiarities; in fact, a true example of 'practice makes perfect'.

In Oporto, some years ago, one of the acknowledged connoisseurs of vintage port was not even in the trade. George Fimister was head of one of the shipping companies which transported port to all the corners of the world. When asked how it was that he had this tremendous knowledge, and seldom erred in placing the year and shipper of a vintage port, his reply was—'I have had the great opportunity and, due to my age, the time to drink a great selection of vintage ports in my lifetime, and I have a good memory.' An honest reply tempered with the humility of the real wine-lover.

Many people wonder how pipe, cigar or cigarette smokers can be professional tasters. The answer is that it depends entirely upon the taster himself, and what he is accustomed to. For instance, it is a known fact that two famous port tasters smoked pipes and cigarettes respectively in their tasting-rooms. No one else could taste at the same time, but when three ladies, heavily scented, appeared one day in one of their tasting-rooms, the bottles were immediately corked, the glasses emptied, and a rather sour remark of 'There will be no more tasting today' proved that something extraneous had entered the room with which they themselves could not compete.

Quality control

The authorities in Oporto, without doubt, see to it that the standards of high quality, maintenance and correct maturation are carried out in the highest degree. The Instituto do Vinho do Porto are entitled to enter at any time the shippers' lodges to inspect them without warning. All new wines made at the vintage are controlled by the Casa do Douro before their departure to Vila Nova de Gaia in the following spring, and these are again examined by the I.V.P. on arrival at this entrepôt.

To become an established port shipper it is necessary to have a minimum stock of three hundred pipes of port in the lodge. The system of shipping rights was established some years ago to force the shippers to maintain a high quality of wines in their lodges, as well as to guarantee the necessary high standard of shipping brands. Possibly the simplest way of explaining this rather complicated system is to give an example of a hypothetical case.

Say Shipping House X held stocks of port in their lodges in Vila Nova de Gaia on 31st December 1972 to the quantity of 6,000 pipes. They also held stocks in the Douro of their 1972 new vintage wines amounting to 3,000 pipes, and in the calendar year of 1971 they had shipped a total of 3,000 pipes. Their shipping rights for 1973 on their stocks in Gaia of 6,000 pipes are at 33 per cent and on their Douro stocks only 30 per cent, which in total amounts to 2,880 pipes. They will not be allowed to ship more than this figure during that year. Now, to obtain these 30 per cent shipping rights on their Douro stock of new 1972 wines, they will have had to produce a quantity equivalent to between 75 per cent and 125 per cent of the previous year's sales—i.e. 1971 sales, which in this case was 3,000 pipes. Should they have produced more than the 125 per cent the excess balance would have only given them 15 per cent shipping rights, while production below the 75 per cent would have had to be worked out by the following formula:

$$\frac{A}{B} \times \frac{30.}{x.}$$

A = 75 per cent of the previous year's sales and B = the actual quantity produced that year. Therefore if only 2,000 pipes had been produced at the 1972 vintage, the formula would produce the following results:

$$\frac{2,250}{2,000} \times \frac{30}{x}, \text{ so } x = \frac{60,000}{2,250}$$

that is, 26·6 per cent or 532 pipes shipping rights.

To produce shipping rights for 1973 equivalent to his 1971 sales, and to maintain a balanced stock, he would have had to make more at the vintage in 1972, at the same time not exceeding the 125 per cent. Shipping rights cannot be exceeded, and when these are expended, all shipping must cease for that year until 1st January of the following year. The answer is intelligent forecasting over a five-year period, but even this can be a problem when one is dealing with Nature. Again, if a shipper transfers or sells any of his stock to another shipper in Vila Nova de Gaia, the quantity involved will be taken as a shipment. In addition an average of 1·8 per cent per annum ullage (loss by evaporation or leakage) should be taken into consideration.

When these regulations came into force in 1957, some shippers were faced with vast capital expenditure in order to build up their stocks to meet the legal requirements, but the situation was slightly eased as they were permitted to borrow through the local *Caixa Geral dos Depositos* by raising loans on their stocks up to a limit of 50 per cent at a very reasonable interest.

Stabilisation

Notwithstanding all these quality and quantity controls, the consumer will still insist on a wine which is brilliant to the last drop, although the natural development of any heavy fortified red wine will be to throw a deposit at some time of its life. To ensure this brilliance, the wine must be fined and stabilised before shipment, and this is most especially true today, when there is a steady increase in original bottling and brand marketing. Naturally, vintage ports and other dated wines are not affected.

Progress in stabilisation has been considerable during the last fifteen years in Gaia, and today most shippers have some sort of stabilisation plants in their lodges. The most popular systems are refrigeration and heat treatment. A previously popular method, ion exchange, has now been forbidden. Stabilisation is generally used for those wines which are fuller and richer in body, having a tendency to throw a deposit and become cloudy after a period of time in bottle, and most especially when they encounter rapid changes of temperature during shipment. A rapid drop in temperature will cause the tartar and the *materia corante* (colouring matter) in the wine to precipitate. Older wines on the other hand, such as old tawnies, have naturally precipitated over the years, while maturing in cask, and the lees formed and deposited are separated from the wine every year when it is racked and aired. Therefore they are automatically much more stable and create few problems when bottled.

The most common method of fining in Gaia is with the use of

gelatine, which will clean the wine completely, but will take out some of the colour and reduce the tannin content. The quantity of gelatine to be used must therefore be accurately judged by the taster, to produce the correct final matching colour of the brand: approximately one-third of tannin to the quantity of gelatine is added to replace the loss. Very occasionally, the whites of eggs are still used for fining the very old tawnies, but bull's blood has now been outmoded. Bentonite is also widely used, and, according to Pacheco Azevedo, it should be added to red wines to assist coagulation. Bentonite is a special montmorillonite clay with great swelling and other colloidal properties.

Both gelatine and bentonite are also used to fine white ports, but in the oenologists' view it is generally undesirable to fine these wines at all, given effective filtration. Fining hastens ageing, precipitation and bottle maturity. In fining, the small particles of suspended material are induced to coalesce and form larger particles which settle out by gravity and carry other suspended matter down with them. Sulphur dioxide is now widely admitted to be a valuable additive at the rate of 55 p.p.m. for tawnies and 50 p.p.m. for rubies. This can be added in any convenient form and is most accurately controlled as a solid. It can be said that very occasionally Spanish clay is used for fining very full-bodied ports, but it is normally only seen in table wine installations.

While refrigeration is now widely used for the stabilisation of port, it is not necessarily one hundred per cent effective in extremely full-bodied young wines, but all the evidence shows that, subject to various controls and safeguards, it still possibly produces the best results. The answer to successful refrigeration is to bottle shortly afterwards with the least possible contact with air.

Stabilisation by refrigeration is carried out by one of two methods: low-temperature storage and the continuous systems. In the first, the temperature of the wine is lowered to between $-5°C$ and $-10°C$, depending upon the strength and fullness of the wine. It is then maintained at that temperature for at least five to ten days, after which it is filtered at that low temperature through a diatomite filter, the most common type used in the port trade. The temperature is then raised to the normal wine temperature of 15°C.

The continuous system of refrigeration allows the temperature of the wine to drop to between —5°C and —10°C. It is next passed through a crystaliser which collects all the tartrates. The wine is then filtered at the low temperature through the diatomite filter, followed immediately by the raising of the temperature to 15°C. The whole process takes approximately an hour, while the first can take anything up to ten days, but we believe that the second method does not give the solid matters time to coagulate sufficiently to enable extraction via the filter.

Heat treatment can also be subdivided into two systems: stabilisation and bacteriological treatment (pasteurisation). The first treatment can be used as a further stabilising factor after refrigeration, as well as a stabiliser on its own. The method used is to raise the temperature of the wine to between 60°C and 70°C, holding that temperature for between 45 seconds and 1 minute, then immediately dropping it to 15°C by means of a cooling system in the machine.

The effectiveness of the second system is governed by speed. The temperature of the wine is raised to between 75°C and 80°C and then dropped very rapidly to 15°C. It is basically a shock treatment, so it is vital that the raising and dropping of the temperature are effected very quickly, the whole treatment taking on an average 1½ minutes. Speed is necessary, as should the wine remain some time at the high temperature, it will acquire a burned 'nose' and be spoiled and useless for blending.

After any stabilisation a light filtration takes place before bottling, virtually a final 'polishing'. However effective the stabilisation process is, every single wine has its own problem, and has to be considered individually. Today, the problem of stability and shelf life is as important as the label and the shape of the bottle, because, whether the shipper likes it or not, the customer is always right, and he insists on the wine being brilliant to the last drop.

Corks

This subject has always been rather ignored and seldom discussed or written about in wine books. The bottle cork, which
is the true epitome of cork itself, is, without doubt, the most
important product of the whole industry. The importance of
first-quality corks for vintage ports, and stopper corks for wood
ports, is vital at all times. A bad cork will ruin a bottle of port.

Cork is made from the bark of the cork oak, *Quercus suber*.
The areas where cork can be economically grown are, in order
of importance, central-southern Portugal and the western
Mediterranean zone, where there is relatively little rain, a great
deal of sun, and also a fairly high level of atmospheric humidity.
The world production is limited to Portugal, Spain, Algeria,
Morocco, Southern France, Italy and Tunisia. Portugal produces some 200,000 tons per annum, which is more than half
the world's crop, so cork is of great importance to Portugal's
trade figures.

The first official rules relating to the protection of cork forests
in Portugal date from the beginning of the fourteenth century.
Portuguese cork has always been distinguished not only by its
great yield but also by its excellence of quality.

The cork oak calls for special treatment owing to the way in
which the crop is harvested. This includes a periodic form of
pruning, aimed principally at maintaining balanced growth,
which is achieved by stripping the bark and giving the tree a
shape which will ensure the maximum yield of cork, and also
ultimately facilitate the stripping of the crop.

Only after the third stripping is the raw cork really adequate
for the production of the bottle cork, about thirty-six years
after the acorn has been planted. In the meantime, the first or
'virgin' stripping can only be used for artistic works such as the
backing of tiles, and when 'shewed up', for walls and insulation.
This latter use is becoming less usual, as other materials are now
being used in its place.

The 'virgin' cork bark is silvery-grey in colour, thick, and
rough on the outside. The colour of the bark of the second

stripping has already become brown, and the roughness has begun to disappear. But as the tree is still growing, the cork is still soft and there is a lot of wastage. However, cork discs can be made from this second stripping to be used inside metal stoppers, and after grinding by machinery, the resultant granules are made into cork boards and other objects.

On reaching the factories the cork is literally cooked in vats of boiling water for some 40–45 minutes to soften it and render it useable for the manufacturers. At the same time any insects, notably ants or other foreign bodies that may be present, will be destroyed by the high temperature of the water. After the boiling and a certain period in store to flatten out the cork sheets, a classification takes place to select the third-stripping sheets for their thickness and quality, and to decide what type of cork stopper will be punched from them. This classification calls for considerable skill and experience, as it includes judging the apertures in the cork itself, the colour, hardness, regularity of growth and porosity. There is an old Portuguese saying: 'There is nothing wasted from cork—it can always be made into something.' But obviously the best must be reserved for wines, etc., and the least amount of wastage must occur, as cork is expensive.

The cutting of the cork sheets was formerly all done by hand, but today, as in most natural products, mechanisation is becoming more and more evident. In former days squares were made direct from the sheets or slabs and smaller pieces, but today these are cut into strips mechanically and then subjected to a cutting operation with a device similar to a punch, the resultant cylinders constituting the cork stopper. The remaining material which is left over is used for grinding or for ornamental purposes.

Once these cylinders or corks have been punched, they are washed in a weak solution of oxalic acid. To produce a white cork, it must be washed with chlorate of lime. The addition of an aniline dye is used for a rose-coloured cork. After washing, the corks are dried in the sun and then are sorted by hand into the various qualities required. This is a complicated affair, owing to the extreme diversity of the types required of every shape and size. To give a few examples, there are champagne-corks, cylindrical and tapered types, stoppers, cask bungs, miniatures and many others with measurements ranging from 2 mm in diameter and 9 mm in height, to the largest bungs of at least 120 mm in diameter and a thickness of 50 mm.

There are other processes that the wine bottle cork may undergo, such as 'hot waxing', which is effected by tumbling the corks in a sealed drum with vaporised paraffin; 'cold waxing', which is a similar process but with blocks of paraffin; and again, other various patented sterile processes.

It is vitally important that the cork adheres to the walls of the container, especially in the case of a bottle, however irregular this might be. It ensures the absolute impermeability of the stopper, and this is explained not only by the force of expansion, of a substance as elastic as cork against the rigid walls of the neck of the bottle, but more particularly by the action of the small cups, formed by the breakage of the surface cells of the cork during the manufacture, which produce a vacuum during the stoppering action, and, in this way, contribute considerably to increasing the adhesion and the resistance to leakage.

As a vegetable product which is completely free from toxic ingredients, the cork stopper does not have any harmful effects on the wines for which it is used. The following two instances rather prove this point. In 1939, a number of vases dating from the third century A.D. were discovered in France; they were stoppered with corks and found to contain wine which, when subjected to tests, was found very suitable for consumption. Again, in Java, some bottles dating from around the year A.D. 600, stoppered with corks, were opened and the wine they contained was in excellent condition.

Besides keeping the qualities of wines and allowing them to breathe in bottle, corks also exert a certain influence in the process of gradual maturation and ageing of the wines. Therefore, only the best selected corks, with ends free from grain, should be used in the bottling of all good wines. Extra-long corks from Catalonia, harder in texture than from any other producing area, are claimed to be unsurpassed for vintage ports.

Mr C. D. Rankin tells an amusing story which occurred when

he was in his cork forests in 1927 with his uncle, Mr John Rankin, or 'Uncle John' as he was known to all his friends. The foreman turned to the latter and asked him what use was the thin piece of cork he had just stripped from the tree, and was given the answer: 'to make discs'. A labourer standing nearby was puzzled and questioned the remark. The foreman then turned to the labourer and asked him if he did not know what a disc was, to which he replied 'Yes, sir, it is a gramophone record!'

7

Shipping, Storing, Decanting and Drinking

Shipping

While I was motoring through Viana do Castelo the other day, the hot July sun gradually sinking into the heat-mist hovering over the horizon, a three-masted schooner suddenly appeared at the mouth of the River Mondego, its sails flapping in a windless sky, slowly edging its way into the small harbour. How different was this scene from that of three hundred years ago when, in this selfsame port, the daily arrival of many such schooners caused continuous hustle and bustle throughout the year and the presence of all nationalities of sailors toing and froing. Today only a few were to be seen, idling around after a good lunch, or mending their nets.

Many trading vessels visited Viana, which, at the end of the seventeenth century was the most important seaport in the north of Portugal. These vessels gathered to load and unload their precious cargoes, which included, at that time, the famous 'Portugal Red Wines'. It was rumoured that many a cask of wine was exchanged for Negro slaves, who had been brought over in the vessels from the North Americas. This appears to be borne out by a young English gentleman Thomas Woodmass, in a letter to his father in September 1704, remarking, 'Oporto is much larger than Viana, and there are more English and Scots families there. The wine of the Douro is much praised by Mr Harris and others. Of the langwidge I know but little, the servants being mostly blacks from America who speak English.'

Large quantities of 'Portugal Red Wine', 'eager wine', or

vinho verde as it is called today, were supplied to the British Naval Commissioners as 'beverage for the sailors'; in the State papers of 10th February 1662, the following entry appears: 'Consul Maynard to the Navy Commissioners. Has sent his bills for beverage wines for the Navy. Asks an order to dispose of the remaining wines, which are spoiling.'

In the course of the years the export of wine from the Minho district ceased, as those produced in the Douro were preferred. Mr Charles Sellers wrote in his book *Oporto Old and New* that it was not possible to discover who was the first Englishman to visit, and possibly settle in Viana, but it was a place of importance, as a British Consul was established there in the seventeenth century. Peter Bearsley, one of the earliest arrivals in Viana, purported to be the pioneer who penetrated the Douro district.

Until about 1730 considerable quantities of red wine were being shipped from Viana, but the greater the increase in shipments of Douro wines, the more Oporto was being used as the port of export, and the less Viana. The sailing vessels gradually changed to steamships, and by the end of the nineteenth century a few large port shippers owned their own vessels. Tides were large, and currents strong and dangerous in the river Douro, and it was only about twenty years ago that a quay was completed to allow ships to go alongside for loading. Formerly, they anchored in the river, looking like busy little mother hens with their chicks clustered around them, as all the loading and unloading was done from lighters of various shapes and sizes. These were first loaded from the shore and then towed out to the ships by tugs, launches or rowing-boats. Now, this has virtually ceased, as not even the larger ships can enter the river, owing to the failure to dredge the barrier of silt, and the low water level caused by the dams being built in the Upper Douro.

Up until very recently, each spring there was a flood when the winter snows melted high in the Spanish mountains and caused the river to rise many metres. This was, in fact, a natural dredging of the river mouth, which no man-made methods have ever been able to emulate. Very often the floods appeared unexpectedly, and within hours small boats and sometimes even larger ships were swept out to sea and lost. Possibly the worst flood was in 1909, when some of the lodges, such as Calem, Sandeman, and Ramos Pinto, situated nearest the river bank in Vila Nova de Gaia, were invaded by the river waters, and empty casks were swept out and seen floating around the narrow streets of Gaia. Losses of wine were light, as the large vats and tightly bunged full casks kept the water out as they kept the wine in. The clearing of the mud and filth after the waters had receded meant much hard work before the lodges were back to normal.

Today, lorries transfer the wine down from the lodges to the main port of Leixões, lying 10 km north of Oporto; and the River Douro is scarcely used for shipments. It is rare to see pipes of port shipped today, as the wine, if not shipped in bottle, will be found in large 2,000-litre metal containers, or even, for wine shipped to the Scandinavian monopolies, in tanker ships; in which case, the wine is pumped straight into the various compartments in the ship. When the port is shipped in bottle, 'dry containers' are used, holding hundreds of cases each.

In Vila Nova de Gaia, every day more and larger TIR lorries are seen manipulating their huge lengths in and out of the narrow streets, eventually arriving at the lodges to receive their cargoes of many thousands of cases of bottled port. Within a few hours these monsters will have disappeared again, heading for their various destinations in Europe. This has great advantages for the distributor, as he knows exactly how much wine he will be receiving on a given day, which minimises his need to hold large stocks.

A certain amount of nostalgia must naturally creep into the story when one recalls stories of the gentle pace of life three hundred years ago, the sailing ships and the time they took to reach their various destinations. But it is also good to remember the quality of the wines shipped in those days compared to the ones today. Port was not the wine we know today. It was vastly inferior, and it was no wonder the Royal Navy was not best pleased with the quality of their 'eager wine', a light and acid wine, similar to the *vinho verde* of today.

In the late 1930s and early 1940s motor cars were seldom used to go to the office and lodges, the roads being well-nigh impassable. Most people took the tram to the river's edge and were then ferried across the river in small rowing-boats, officially registered as ferries. The river at this point, adjacent to the large double bridge leading to Gaia, was very busy. All the wine was loaded at this quay and there were permanent comings and goings of all forms of craft. The boatmen had their own philosophy, they felt that every boat or hazard would remove itself from their path, or they could circumvent it without difficulty.

One day, as the author was being rowed across, we had to row under some hawsers, holding a ship about to leave. The boatman had not noticed the pilot-boat alongside, nor had he realised the boat was about to leave. When this was pointed out to him, he replied with his special brand of philosophy: 'There are no hazards, do not preoccupy yourself.' At that moment the hawsers were released, and we found ourselves within a metre of the rudder and propeller. The boatman still could not understand what all the fuss was about, when suddenly the propeller started churning up the water and soaked both of us to the skin. To the accompaniment of a stream of abuse from the author, in good colloquial Portuguese, describing the boatman and his antecedents in no mean terms, he manoeuvred his boat with great skill and somehow avoided fouling the propeller; then he quietly replied, 'Your Excellency, it seems impossible!' What could one say? Imperturbably, he continued the crossing and his passenger was deposited, wet but otherwise unharmed, on the quay to continue his way to the office.

Storing

Writing on this subject, we are thinking principally about the storing and keeping of vintage ports, as we still believe that bottle age does not normally improve wood ports, especially old tawnies, which have spent their natural life maturing in cask. However, we concede that some young rubies do appear to soften down after some time in bottle. There is no need to cosset port, as it is a naturally strong wine, and has been 'brought up' to withstand many varied climates and conditions in various corners of the world. Its very birth is a difficult one because of the schistous soil and the extreme climatic conditions in the Douro valley, so it will not object too strongly to some rough treatment in its life, so long as this is not too prolonged.

The following story rather proves this point. Some bottles of vintage port were left in a garage during the air-raids over England in 1940, when the owner had had to leave in a hurry. Five years later, when the war was over, the owner returned and was delighted to discover that the bottles were in perfect condition and the wine had continued to mature and improve normally. Possibly the furniture, trunks, broken tiles and bricks had kept them insulated during that long period? Not that we advocate this type of storage, as sudden changes of temperature do not help the maturation of any wine.

If vintage port is stored with your wine merchant, from whom you purchased it, it will remain in his cellars under ideal conditions until you need it. Usually a storage rent is charged for this. But if you are lucky enough to own an older house with a cellar, there is no problem; a modern house can give rise to problems, though, as space has to be found where a moderate temperature can be maintained, with no draughts and the least amount of light. Today it is possible to find excellent wine racks of various designs and prices to fit any size or area you wish to select as your 'cellar', which slightly eases the situation.

We do *not* advocate keeping the vintage bottle in an upright position, as, after many years, the corks will become dry, having had no contact with the wine. When the bottles are originally filled, a splash of white paint is placed on one side, and the bottle should be laid down in the rack or bin with this mark uppermost. This is important, as should the wine be moved at any time during its life, the owner will always know which way up to replace the bottles so that the crust, which will be falling and forming, remains in the same place.

Normally, a vintage port bottle is waxed, but today some shippers use the new composition capsule, which is equally efficient and does not create as many complications, such as

cracked sealing wax, and the rather messy business of removing it when decanting. The reason for using both wax and
the composition capsule is to prevent the *Oronico flavius* wine
fly from laying its eggs on the cork, which will gradually
destroy it. The fly only appears on a wet cork or one that
has been 'weeping', as it feeds on the natural sugar of the wine
and it will, if allowed, eat through the whole cork until it
reaches the wine itself, where it will have a beautiful death by
drowning.

Wax is an ancient expedient, but the composition capsule has
only relatively recently been produced. During transit, rough
handling of a case of port may result in broken or cracked wax.
Should the quality of wax not be up to standard, it can become
brittle and break easily. So long as the cork is dry, there should
be no danger of the fly attacking it, and generally this is so, as,
when bottling, the top of the cork is dried, then a dab of sealing
wax is placed on this, which in turn is again allowed to dry
completely before finally the entire neck of the bottle is dipped
into hot wax. So even should the outside wax be cracked or
broken, the original dab underneath will still be intact. Some
shippers use the ordinary metal capsule, which we personally
do not advocate, as eventually the lead will eat through the
aluminium lining, producing a sticky white substance which
appears on the top of the bottle. A new capsule should then be
fitted after the neck has been wiped and cleaned.

Decanting and glasses

There seems to be some magic surrounding the word 'decanting',
and many people shudder with fear at even attempting this
really very simple operation. There are only two things one
must remember the whole time. The first is that as the wine
should have been lying down in one position for a long time, it
should be treated as gently and reverently as possible. Secondly,
the slower it is decanted, the greater the resultant quantity of
clear wine from each bottle. (You may notice the author's
Scottish feelings about this.)

The simplest adage of when to decant is 'the older the port, the nearer the meal'. This is only commonsense, as a very old 50- or 60-year vintage port, once opened, and allowed to come in contact with the air, will lose the beautiful bouquet much more rapidly than, say, a 10-year-old one, which actually needs this contact to allow it to breathe and 'expand'.

Ideally, if time is available, take the bottle from the rack gently and slowly, and stand it upright for twenty-four hours before decanting. This will allow any of the soft crust, deposit, or, in a very old wine, some of the loose crust hardened with great age, to fall slowly to the bottom of the bottle and settle. Have the necessary implements at hand ready for the 'ceremony', which is really very simple. You need a corkscrew, a candle, some form of filter, a decanter or a completely clean bottle or container, and a clean glass. Try and find a corkscrew without the usual sharp edge to the actual screw, which will always cut the cork and act more as a gimlet, especially when the cork is old and slightly soft. If possible, a long one would be best, as you will remember that the vintage port cork is longer than the normal one. The candle is not essential but we recommend it, as it gives the perfect light for showing the clarity of a wine, purely due to the shape of the flame. The perfect filter is the silver, hook-nosed one with minute holes, but these are few and far between, so the more mundane muslin, completely neutral in smell, and well washed, can be used. It has even been suggested that ladies' nylon stockings (unused) are equally good.

First remove the wax or capsule with a heavy knife and clean the top of the bottle. Draw the cork slowly and, should this break, try to remove as much of it as possible before starting to tilt the bottle slowly, always with the white splash uppermost, and begin pouring. If you are lucky enough to have one of those hook-nosed strainers, you will notice the reason for this hook, which is to allow the wine to flow quietly down the side of the bottle instead of splashing into the centre and possibly forming a froth. Place a lighted candle in such a position as to have the flame just below the shoulder of the bottle, so that you can see the movement of the wine and crust as you continue pouring.

Tilt the bottle as slowly as possible, so as to obtain the maximum of clear wine.

When eventually the wine appears to be muddy, or the crust is falling out into the strainer or muslin, it is wiser to stop pouring, but you can now continue to do this into a glass. In an exceptionally old vintage port, you will find that the crust is so hard, and so completely adhered to the side of the bottle, that possibly every drop of the liquid will be crystal clear. In younger vintages, obviously the deposit is not so firm, and more care will have to be taken. It must be remembered that the final dregs you pour into the glass is still port, and can be used for cooking.

Once you have decanted the wine, taste it, and see that it is clean and sound. Then, depending upon its age, allow it to breathe or not, by leaving the stopper of the decanter out for a period of time. It is very difficult to give this time exactly, as all vintages differ so much. In the case of a very old one we would advise you to place the stopper immediately in the decanter, thus preserving all the beauties stored up for so many years in the bottle, allowing it to breathe for only a few minutes. Here we are talking about 50-year-old wines. A 10- or 15-year-old vintage, on the other hand, could need some hours of breathing before drinking, in some cases four to five hours. As there cannot be any laid-down rules on this subject, we would suggest that once the wine is decanted, and the stopper has been left out, you should check the wine and see how it is developing in the room.

The other method of decanting is no longer practical, but may be used to show off before guests! It entails the removal of the neck of the bottle by the use of hot tongs. These special metal tongs are heated to a cherry red, placed just under the flange of the neck of the bottle, and after half to one minute, when the glow has gone, the tongs are removed. A wet rag is then applied to the neck of the bottle and a sharp movement will break this cleanly and easily, thus eliminating the necessity of drawing the cork.

During early maturation in bottle, vintage port goes through some periods of being 'out of condition'. These normally occur either in the spring or autumn, possibly caused by the natural development of the wine provoked by the seasonal temperature variations.

The throwing of the crust in the bottle is equivalent to the more rapid process of depositing the lees in the casks. All vintage port bottles used to be cleaned with chipped copper wire, whose sharp points and edges very slightly roughened up the inside of the bottle and thus helped the formation of a firm crust which would not slip. The crust is harsh and bitter to the taste. There is a story of a maidservant in a large country mansion, some years ago, who went to her master's wine merchant to purchase for herself a bottle of port 'the same as her master always drunk'. It happened to be a very old vintage port, unknown to her, and far from decanting it, she and her colleagues poured this delectable wine straight into glasses, and had a party. When she returned some time afterwards to purchase another bottle of the same wine, the wine merchant asked her how she had enjoyed it, and was shocked to realise that she had not decanted it. Her reply was that she thought it was very good, as did her friends, and in fact, even the 'little hard bits' which were left over at the bottom, had been exceedingly good on toast and butter the following morning at breakfast!

Very occasionally one hears of the expression 'beeswing'. This is that part of the deposit or crust which is formed of the mucilage, that is, the gummy tissue which separates the little cells or sacs of sugar and water that make up the grape. The grape is not merely a bag of juice within a skin, but a highly composite agglomeration. Beeswing has no value except as a guarantee of age, for it takes many years for this substance to detach itself and form the delicate, greasy film which is prized. The detached beeswing is of a purely vegetable composition, as distinguished from lees and crust, which contain mineral salts.

Rubies, tawnies and white ports need no decanting, nor do they need special treatment or storage, as they remain in the cask until they are shipped.

Fully to appreciate any port you need to use a decent-sized glass partially filled, rather than a small glass completely filled.

The latter makes it wellnigh impossible to appreciate the colour or the bouquet; not to mention the extra hazard of transferring it to your mouth with a shaky hand and risking ruining the

dinner table or your clothes by spillage! There is a recommended port glass, a tulip-shaped one with a medium-sized stem, rather like a small version of a claret glass.

The gout myth exploded

Firmly fixed in the mind of man is the connection between port wine and gout. We must dispel this fallacy without more ado. In the Georgian and Victorian era, prodigious quantities of food and wine were consumed, as were large quantities of port. When people were then troubled with gout they immediately related it to the port, as port was the last thing they remembered imbibing. In fact, gout is a painful condition of the joints caused by a high uric acid content in the body, and is caused variously by excessive exercise or consumption of goods with a high acid content, such as most forms of offal or strawberries, to name just a few. Wines, too, may well be a contributory factor, but not the cause. Gout, however, is scarcely known among port shippers in Oporto, and as a group, we do our share of port-drinking. So this painful disease cannot be blamed on port.

Luckily for the trade, the Americans decided to do some research on this subject. The investigation in 1953 by Dr Friedman and his research associates was organised simply to 'prove or disprove the age-old belief that gout is caused by port wine'. The wine was first administered to experimental animals in amounts equal to 6 per cent of their body-weight each day. 'This would be equivalent,' Dr Friedman said, 'to a man drinking about four quarts a day.' (An American quart is a little less than a litre, but more than a bottle.) Next, healthy young adults were given port wine in amounts of one quart per day for at least six weeks and, like the laboratory animals, showed no symptoms of gout. Nor did the treatment produce even any detectable increase in the production of uric acid, the chemical which is deposited in joints to cause the excruciating pain of gout. Next, known gout sufferers were fed a quart of port wine daily without the wines producing any effect upon the disease. 'Daily ingestion of port wine, even in large quantities,' the medical researchers concluded, 'has no detectable influence on gout.' An independent report by Dr Ephraim Engleman of the University of California expressed a like conclusion: 'No wine has any relationship with causing or increasing the severity of gout.'

To conclude this small dissertation on gout, it would be appropriate to quote Dr Richardson, who said: 'If port wine does not agree with you, there is something the matter with *you*, not with the port; the use of port wine is, therefore, a good criterion of health.'

Port is often blamed for the 'morning after the night before' headache. The sufferer of this headache has nearly always forgotten the odd apéritif, the white wine with the fish, followed by red wine, then port and possibly a final nightcap before leaving the party. It is a compliment to the wine that he remembers he drank port, but a tragedy that he blames his hangover on this beautiful wine, solely because it is the dessert wine in Britain and therefore the last wine to be served. Possibly, port being a conversational wine, tongues are loosened and the port decanter has been sent round rather more often than is good for anyone, thus apportioning some blame on this wine.

When to drink port

In various countries of the world we are asked many times, 'When should one drink port?' The answer, very briefly is 'as and when you wish'. It was always said that in Britain, port was served as a dessert wine and it gained a reputation of being drunk only in London clubs by elderly colonels. It would surprise many people to know that, in the immediate years before the Second World War, Britain imported nearly 60 per cent of the total port trade, and 80 per cent of this quantity was drunk in the pubs, generally as 'port and lemon'. At the same time, it was a recommended tonic to be taken mid-morning and, as one dear old Scottish lady was heard to say, 'I never touch alcohol, but a wee glass of port with my Dundee cake does me good!'

In 1963 the French became the largest importers of port in the world. For the first time in the history of the wine Great Britain dropped behind. The French drink it solely as an apéritif, preferring cognac with their coffee. In Portugal, dry white port, well chilled or on the rocks with a twist of lemon peel, is a most popular apéritif, and old tawnies are generally preferred to vintage ports as dessert wines. Port and soda-water, as a long drink in summer, is a good thirst-quencher, and you will often see the port shippers, in their vineyards, during the vintage, taking this splendid cool drink, to the astonishment of their visitors. We then remind them that it is not far from the 'port and lemon' which the British found so appetising and refreshing. But for such mixed drinks it is only sensible to use the cheaper ports.

Over 90 per cent of the total production of vintage port is drunk in Britain. This wine, we suggest, should be drunk as a dessert wine, preferably when there is plenty of time to linger at the table, and really appreciate and savour its unique qualities. It should be pointed out to those present that the wine has been many, many years maturing to reach its peak of perfection, and they would be well advised not to pollute the atmosphere by smoking either cigarettes or cigars at least until the first glass has been finished. In this way the full fragrance of the wine can be fully appreciated.

It is a known stimulating and amusing game, evolved by the shippers, that one and all should try and guess the year of the wine and the shipper, when vintage port is served. On one occasion, when dining with a well-known port connoisseur, the great moment of broaching the first decanter of vintage port had arrived. The honoured guest was asked to guess the year and shipper, and, after due hesitation, he achieved this difficult deduction successfully. Immediately compliments flowed both from the host and the guests. When the second decanter of a still older wine was produced and was guessed correctly by the same gentleman, the hushed audience was truly dumbfounded. However, his honesty spoiled his reputation by his adding— 'Of course, I may have been influenced by the fact that I happened to come into the dining-room shortly before dinner and saw the slips of paper which your butler had tied on the decanters!'

What does one eat with port? To quote the late Mr Wm. J. Todd, 'Perhaps new walnuts (with a self-sacrificing daughter or niece at hand to remove the skins) are the best accompaniment. Cheese (if not too bolshevist a nature) prepares the palate.' Not everyone agrees with his views. As port is a fortified sweet wine, one immediately thinks of cheese. But how many types of cheese are there in the world? Blue, goat, peppery, garlic, herbs, cream, hard, soft, in fact hundreds of varieties in different countries. Stilton is considered the best 'marriage', but some find that this is too strong for vintage port, and they prefer nuts with this wine, both brazils and walnuts, young or old, and reserve this cheese for tawnies. Possibly the British hard cheeses are the best choice for both types of port, such as genuine Cheddar and Cheshire. And here again, the choice is fantastic.

There is an old saying in the port trade: 'Buy on an apple and sell on cheese'—a very good tip to remember, as the apple will clean the palate completely, and when buying, any doubt about the wine will be accentuated, while the cheese will always enhance the wine.

As a 'starter' to a meal, port and melon is often served, but if the melon is sweet and ripe, it is a pity to pour the port on to it, and preferably it should be drunk with it. Nuts, undoubtedly, are always a perfect accompaniment as well as dried figs, and, even better, split a dried fig and insert some pieces of walnut or an almond. Again, port is often served with a fruit salad, but here one must be more careful because tangerines and oranges will ruin the taste of the wine.

It is not true to say that port must be accompanied by food that is dry and not sweet as, some time ago, when one had the great pleasure of lunching with the old-established wine merchants in Great Britain, very often a delicious fruit cake was served after the cheese with the port—either vintage or old tawny—or both. Thankfully, everybody has his own taste, and this is very personal, but we would suggest that pepper and garlic cheeses should be avoided with port, as well as fresh citrus fruits.

Perhaps the ceremony of drinking port at the Factory House or British Association, in Oporto, can best show the perfect way. Here, in this large building of solid granite, there are two dining-rooms of identical size with intercommunicating doors. The tables in both dining-rooms, each seating a maximum of forty-two guests, are identical. The first is the 'eating' room, covered by one single double-damask table cloth. We call this the eating-room, because, when dinner is finished, a glass of old tawny is served before rising from the table; this is not a signal for speeches or toasts, it is solely to 'clean the palate' before moving into the second and adjoining room. Thus the dreadful port trade expression of a non-vintage port, 'mouth-wash', was born!

The guests then rise, the doors are opened, and, not forgetting one's napkin (a very serious offence!), they file through and sit at identical places at a highly-polished table, decorated usually with red roses, and laden with both dried and fresh fruits, almonds, walnuts and brazils. The communicating doors are then closed so as to prevent any smells of food entering. A truly beautiful sight: only candles flickering and picking out the lights on the crystal decanters of vintage port, a wondrous array of colour. Here the royal and other toasts are proposed and drunk, speeches made, and the perfect evening, seldom to be experienced in the modern world today, continues long into the night. After a reasonable time the ladies rise, and leave the gentlemen to continue with their smoking, their stories, and their 'conversational' port.

In summer we advocate that port, either red or white, should be slightly chilled (but *not* vintage port) as warm port is possibly as unpleasant a drink as warm beer.

There are many traditions attached to port and its drinking. Possibly the most discussed and best known is that of passing the port round the table, always to the left. The host, after pouring a very small quantity into his own glass first, is allowed to serve the lady on his right and left, so long as the decanter or bottle does not leave his hand. The decanter is then passed on to the left, the gentleman usually serving the lady as sometimes the decanters are very heavy. Should the decanter stop too long at someone's elbow, a gentle reminder from the thirstier guests, such as 'Mr X, your "passport" is out of order', or 'do you know the Bishop of so-and-so, he *never* passed the port', will cause the wine to be circulated again, as no glass should ever be left empty. Another well-known cry of despair is 'please polish the table', as usually the bottom of the coaster is covered in green baize, and the host will then explain that the table is only polished properly when the port is pushed round in its coaster regularly.

There have been many and varied stories of how the leftward-passing tradition started. Some say it originated in the Royal Navy, the word 'port' meaning 'left', or that the clockwise direction caused by passing to the left, is 'the natural way of the sun'. But it is generally agreed that it was evolved through sheer commonsense, as most people are right-handed and it is easier to pass wine that way than any other. These traditions are much loved and give a certain mystique to this great wine. But we affirm that we have never hesitated for one moment to drink port, from any sort of container, at shoots, picnics, on the beach, or at any time, whether served from the left or the right!

Longevity is also attributed to port-drinkers, as shown by a story told by the late Mr Frank Yeatman, of Taylor, Fladgate and Yeatman, many years ago while we were sipping our port after the weekly luncheon at the Factory House. He had recently returned from his medical check-up in London, which he had every two or three years. As his doctor was away on leave, a young locum attended him and after the examination he put some rather personal questions to him. He found him in such excellent health for his age, which was then over eighty, that the first question was whether he ate or drank very much, to which Mr Yeatman replied 'just normally'. Again when asked what he drank the reply was 'obviously, port'. The locum then plucked up his courage to ask the third question, which was a little more personal: 'And could you tell me, sir, how much port do you drink in a year on an average?' The reply was immediate: 'About a pipe, or in the layman's language, seven hundred and twenty bottles approximately.' All present at the table immediately began to do their homework and, calculating the port trade's measure of six good glasses to the bottle, agreed this would be 'about normal'.

We should like to end with a very personal quotation. 'The Good Lord gives us the soil, the vines, the weather, and the grapes, and it is up to us, the producers, to do our utmost to produce the wine in such a way as to give it its due reverence.'

Appendix 1

Vintage Ports and their Shippers, 1869–1970

Adams, 1935, 1945, 1947, 1948, 1950, 1955, 1960, 1963, 1966
Barros, Almeida, 1943, 1970
Borges, 1914, 1922, 1963, 1970
Burmester, 1873, 1878, 1887, 1890, 1896, 1900, 1904, 1908, 1912, 1920, 1922, 1927, 1931, 1935, 1937, 1940, 1943, 1948, 1954, 1955, 1958, 1960, 1963, 1970
Butler, Nephew, 1922, 1924, 1927, 1934, 1942, 1945, 1948, 1955, 1957, 1958, 1960, 1970
Cálem & Filho, 1935, 1947, 1948, 1955, 1958, 1960, 1963, 1970
Cockburn Smithes, 1870, 1872, 1873, 1875, 1878, 1881, 1884, 1887, 1890, 1894, 1896, 1900, 1904, 1908, 1912, 1927, 1935, 1947, 1950, 1955, 1960, 1963, 1967, 1970
Croft, 1870, 1872, 1875, 1878, 1881, 1884, 1885, 1887, 1890, 1894, 1896, 1897, 1900, 1904, 1908, 1912, 1917, 1920, 1922, 1924, 1927, 1935, 1942, 1945, 1950, 1955, 1960, 1963, 1966, 1970
Douro Wine Shippers' & Growers' Association, 1970
Da Silva, A. J. (now Quintado Noval-Vinhos S.A.R.L.) 1896, 1900, 1904, 1908, 1912, 1917, 1919, 1920, 1923, 1927, 1931, 1934, 1941, 1942, 1945, 1947, 1950, 1955, 1958, 1960, 1963, 1966, 1970
Da Silva, C., 1970
Delaforce, 1870, 1873, 1875, 1878, 1881, 1884, 1887, 1890, 1894, 1896, 1900, 1904, 1908, 1912, 1917, 1919, 1920, 1927, 1935, 1945, 1947, 1950, 1955, 1958, 1960, 1963, 1966, 1970
Dixon, 1884, 1887, 1890
Diez Hermanos, 1970
Dow, 1870, 1872, 1873, 1875, 1878, 1881, 1884, 1887, 1890, 1892, 1896, 1899, 1904, 1908, 1912, 1920, 1924, 1927, 1934
Dow–Silva & Cosens, 1945, 1947, 1950, 1955, 1960, 1963, 1966, 1970
Feist, 1922, 1970

Ferreira, A. A., 1894, 1896, 1897, 1900, 1904, 1908, 1912, 1917, 1920, 1924, 1937

Ferreira, A. A. Sucrs., 1945, 1955, 1960, 1965, 1966, 1970

Feuerheerd, 1870, 1872, 1873, 1875, 1878, 1881, 1884, 1887, 1890, 1894, 1896, 1900, 1904, 1908, 1912, 1917, 1920, 1924, 1927, 1942, 1943, 1945, 1951, 1955

Fonseca, 1870, 1873, 1878, 1881, 1884, 1887, 1890, 1896, 1900, 1904, 1908, 1912, 1920, 1922, 1927, 1934

Guimaraens & Co, 1945*, 1948*, 1955*, 1958, 1960*, 1963, 1966, 1970

Gonzalez Byass, 1896, 1900, 1904, 1908, 1912, 1917, 1920, 1945, 1955, 1960, 1963, 1967, 1970

Gould Campbell, 1870, 1872, 1873, 1875, 1878, 1881, 1884, 1885, 1887, 1890, 1896, 1900, 1904, 1908, 1912, 1920, 1922, 1924, 1934, 1942, 1955, 1960, 1963, 1966

Graham, 1870, 1872, 1873, 1875, 1878, 1880, 1881, 1884, 1885, 1887, 1890, 1892, 1894, 1896, 1897, 1901, 1904, 1908, 1912, 1917, 1920, 1924, 1927, 1935, 1942, 1945, 1948, 1955, 1960, 1963, 1966, 1970

Hutcheson & Ca Lda, 1970

Kingston, 1922, 1924, 1927

Kopke, 1870, 1872, 1873, 1875, 1878, 1881, 1884, 1887, 1890, 1892, 1894, 1896, 1897, 1900, 1904, 1908, 1912, 1917, 1919, 1920, 1922, 1926, 1927, 1935, 1945, 1948, 1950, 1952, 1955, 1958, 1960, 1963, 1965†, 1966, 1970

Mackenzie, 1870, 1873, 1875, 1878, 1881, 1884, 1887, 1890, 1896, 1900, 1904, 1908, 1912, 1919, 1920, 1922, 1927, 1935, 1945, 1948, 1950, 1952, 1954, 1955, 1957, 1958, 1960, 1963, 1966, 1970

Martinez Gassiot, 1870, 1872, 1873, 1874, 1875, 1878, 1880, 1881, 1884, 1885, 1886, 1887, 1890, 1892, 1894, 1896, 1897, 1900, 1904, 1908, 1911, 1912, 1919, 1922, 1927, 1931, 1934, 1945, 1955, 1958, 1960, 1963, 1967, 1970

Messias, 1970

Morgan, 1870, 1872, 1873, 1875, 1878, 1881, 1884, 1887, 1890, 1894, 1896, 1900, 1904, 1908, 1912, 1920, 1922, 1924, 1927, 1942, 1948, 1955, 1960, 1963, 1966, 1970

Niepoort, 1927, 1945, 1970

Offley Forrester, 1870, 1872, 1873, 1874, 1875, 1878, 1881, 1884, 1885, 1887, 1888, 1890, 1892, 1894, 1896, 1897, 1900, 1902, 1904, 1908,

* Shipped under Fonseca label.   † Not shipped to U.K.

1910, 1912, 1919, 1920, 1921, 1922, 1923, 1924, 1925, 1927, 1929, 1931, 1934, 1935, 1942, 1950, 1954, 1958, 1960, 1962, 1966, 1967, 1970
Osborne, 1970
Quarles Harris, 1927, 1934, 1945, 1947, 1950, 1955, 1958, 1960, 1963, 1966, 1970
Manuel D. Poças, 1967, 1970
Ramos Pinto, 1924, 1927, 1945, 1955, 1970
Real Vinicola (Quinta do Sibio), 1945, 1947, 1950, 1955, 1960, 1970
Rebello Valente, 1870, 1875, 1878, 1881, 1884, 1887, 1890, 1892, 1894, 1896, 1897, 1900, 1904, 1908, 1911, 1912, 1917, 1920, 1922, 1924, 1927, 1935, 1960, 1963, 1966
Robertson Bros, 1942, 1945, 1947, 1955, 1970
Royal Oporto Wine Co, 1934, 1945, 1970
Sandeman, 1870, 1872, 1873, 1875, 1878, 1880, 1881, 1884, 1887, 1890, 1892, 1894, 1896, 1897, 1900, 1904, 1908, 1911, 1912, 1917, 1920, 1924, 1927, 1934, 1935, 1942, 1945, 1947, 1950, 1955, 1958, 1960, 1963, 1966, 1967, 1970
Smith Woodhouse, 1870, 1872, 1873, 1875, 1878, 1880, 1881, 1884, 1887, 1890, 1896, 1897, 1900, 1904, 1908, 1912, 1917, 1920, 1924, 1927, 1935, 1945, 1947, 1950, 1955, 1960, 1963, 1966, 1970
Sociedade Constantino, 1912, 1927, 1935, 1941, 1945, 1947, 1950, 1958, 1966
Southard, 1927
Stormont Tait, 1896, 1900, 1904, 1908, 1912, 1920, 1922, 1927
Taylor, Fladgate & Yeatman, 1870, 1872, 1873, 1875, 1878, 1880, 1881, 1884, 1887, 1890, 1892, 1896, 1900, 1904, 1906, 1908, 1912, 1917, 1920, 1924, 1927, 1935, 1938, 1940, 1942, 1945, 1948, 1955, 1960, 1963, 1966, 1967, 1970
Tuke Holdsworth,
Hunt Roope & Co, 1870, 1873, 1874, 1875, 1881, 1884, 1887, 1890, 1892, 1896, 1900, 1904, 1906, 1908, 1912, 1917, 1920, 1922, 1924, 1927, 1934, 1935, 1943, 1945, 1947, 1950, 1955, 1960, 1963, 1966
Van Zellers, 1878, 1881, 1884, 1887, 1890, 1892, 1896, 1904, 1908, 1912, 1917, 1922, 1924, 1927, 1935
Vieira de Souza, 1970
Warre, 1870, 1872, 1875, 1878, 1881, 1884, 1887, 1890, 1894, 1896,

1900, 1904, 1908, 1912, 1917, 1920, 1922, 1924, 1927, 1934, 1947, 1950,
1955, 1958, 1960, 1963, 1966, 1970,
Wiese & Krohn, 1927, 1934, 1970

Note: most vintages from 1938 to 1945 inclusive were bottled in
Oporto.

1975 Vintage. At the time of printing the 1975's have been declared as a
Vintage by many Houses, but it is too early to comment on them as
complete information was not available at the time of going to press.

Appendix 2

Exports of Port, 1958–1975

(All quantities in hectolitres)

Year	Container	Cask	Bottle	Total
1958	203	195,384	17,357	212,944
1959	75	212,781	17,631	230,487
1960	128	210,782	19,446	230,356
1961	113	249,116	19,726	268,955
1962	109	249,030	20,351	269,490
1963	73	242,361	20,461	262,895
1964	7,864	248,293	19,790	275,947
1965	32,093	261,073	18,548	311,714
1966	48,587	243,151	22,422	314,160
1967	65,734	213,107	21,944	300,785
1968	90,322	213,899	27,270	331,491
1969	121,891	169,776	29,959	321,626
1970	160,053	148,466	42,012	350,531
1971	196,591	120,616	50,964	368,171
1972	245,371	116,989	72,586	434,946
1973	282,551	92,649	100,707	475,907
1974	282,929	45,771	104,386	433,086
1975	254,510	27,444	97,538	379,492

Appendix 3

Duties on Port Imported into the United Kingdom, 1921–1976

From	To	Duty per imperial gallon (4·55 litres) in bulk	Duty per gallon in bottle
——	April 1921	3/–	—
April 1921	April 1927	6/–	—
April 1927	Sept. 1939	8/–	—
Sept. 1939	July 1940	12/–	—
July 1940	April 1942	16/–	—
April 1942	April 1943	28/–	—
April 1943	Nov. 1947	34/–	37/6
Nov. 1947	April 1948	44/–	47/6
April 1948	April 1958	50/–	52/6
April 1958	April 1960	38/–	40/6
April 1960	July 1961	26/–	28/6
July 1961	April 1964	27/6	30/–
April 1964	April 1965	30/6	33/–
April 1965	July 1966	36/6	39/–
July 1966	March 1968	39/3	41/9
March 1968	Nov. 1968	45/3	47/9
Nov. 1968	April 1973	54/3	56/9
April 1973	July 1973	£1·975	£2·100
July 1973	Jan. 1974	£1·875	£1·975
Jan. 1974	March 1974	£1·775	£1·850
March 1974	Jan. 1975	£2·320	£2·395
Jan. 1975	April 1975	£2·220	£2·270
April 1975	Jan. 1976	£3·550	£3·60

Appendix 4

List of Port Shippers

A. A. Cálem & Filho Lda
A. P. Santos & Ca Lda
Adolfo de Oliveira & Ca
Adriano Ramos Pinto-Vinhos (S.A.R.L.)
Alberto Castro Lança Lda
Barros, Almeida & Ca
Butler, Nephew & Co
C. N. Kopke & Ca Lda
C. da Silva-Vinhos (S.A.R.L.)
Cockburn Smithes & Ca Lda
Companhia Agricola e Comercial dos Vinhos do Porto
Companhia Geral da Agricultura das Vinhas do Alto Douro
Croft & Ca Lda
Delaforce Sons & Ca-Vinhos (S.A.R.L.)
Diez Hermanos Lda
Feuerheerd Bros & Ca Lda
Gilberts & Ca Lda
Gonzalez Byass & Co
Guimaraens-Vinhos (S.A.R.L.)
H. & C. J. Feist-Vinhos (S.A.R.L.)
Hutcheson & Ca Lda
J. Carvalho Macedo Lda
J. H. Andresen, Sucrs Lda
J. W. Burmester & Ca Lda
M. C. da Costa Oliveira
Mackenzie & Ca Lda
Manoel D. Poças Junior Lda
Manuel R. d'Assumpção & Filhos Lda
Martinez Gassiot & Co Ltd

Morgan Bros Lda
Niepoort & Ca Lda
Offley Forrester-Vinhos (S.A.R.L.)
Osborne (Vinhos de Portugal) & Ca Lda
Pinto Pereira Lda
Quarles Harris & Ca Lda
Quinta do Noval-Vinhos (S.A.R.L.)
Real Companhia Vinícola do Norte de Portugal (S.A.R.L.)
Robertson Bros. & Ca Lda
Rodrigues Pinho & Ca Lda
Rozès Lda
Sandeman & Ca Lda
Serafim Cabral Lda
Silva & Cosens Ltd
Smith Woodhouse & Ca Lda
Sociedade Agrícola e Comercial dos Vinhos Messias (S.A.R.L.)
Sociedade dos Vinhos do Alto Corgo Lda
Sociedade dos Vinhos Borges & Irmão (S.A.R.L.)
Sociedade dos Vinhos do Porto Constantino Lda
Taylor, Fladgate & Yeatman-Vinhos (S.A.R.L.)
The Douro Wine Shippers' and Growers' Association Lda
Vieira de Sousa & Ca
W. & J. Graham & Co
Warre & Ca Lda
Wiese & Krohn, Sucrs Lda

Select Bibliography

Allen, H. Warner: *Sherry and Port* (London 1952)
The History of Wine (London 1961)
Banco Borges & Irmão: *Estudos Sectorais (Vinho do Porto)* (Oporto 1973)
Bradford, Sarah: *The Englishman's Wine* (London 1969)
Carwardine, Peter A.: *A Study of the Port Wine Trade* (private paper)
Cobb, Gerald: *Oporto Older and Newer* (1965)
Cockburn, Ernest: *Port Wine and Oporto* (London n.d.)
Couche, Donald D.: *Modern Detection and Treatment of Wine Diseases and Defects* (London 1935)
Forrester, Baron Joseph James: *Papers relating to the Improvement of the Navigation of the River Douro* (Oporto 1844)
A Word or Two on Port Wine (London 1844)
Observations on the Attempts lately made to reform the Abuses practised in Portugal in the Making and Treatment of Port Wine (London 1845)
The Oliveira Prize Essay on Portugal (London 1853)
Fisher, H. E.: *The Portugal Trade* (London 1969)
Fundo de Fomento de Exportação e Junta Nacional de Cortiça: *Cork Comes from Portugal* (Lisbon n.d.)
Hogg, Anthony: *Wine Mine* (London n.d.)
Jeffs, Julian: *Wines of Europe* (London 1971)
Leslie, Francis S.: *From Port to Port* (Glasgow 1946—pamphlet)
Moreira da Fonseca, Engenheiro Agrónomo Alvaro Baltazar: *As Demarcaçoes Pombalinas no Douro Vinhateiro* (Oporto 1951)
Companhia Geral da Agricultura das Vinhas do Alto Douro (Oporto 1955)
Ordish, George: *The Great Wine Blight* (London 1972)
Read, Jan: *The Wines of Spain and Portugal* (London 1973)
Sanceau, Elaine: *The British Factory—Oporto* (Barcelos 1970)

179

Sellers, Charles: *Oporto Old and New* (London 1899)
Simon, André L: *Port* (London 1934)
Symington, John D.: *Portugal, The Ancient Alliance* (Oporto 1960)
Todd, William J.: *Port* (London 1926)
Vinho do Porto, Instituto do: *Regulations Governing the Description of Special Types of Port Wine* (Oporto 1973)

Index